UNBROKEN POETRY

THE WORK OF ENRIQUE MARTINEZ CELAYA

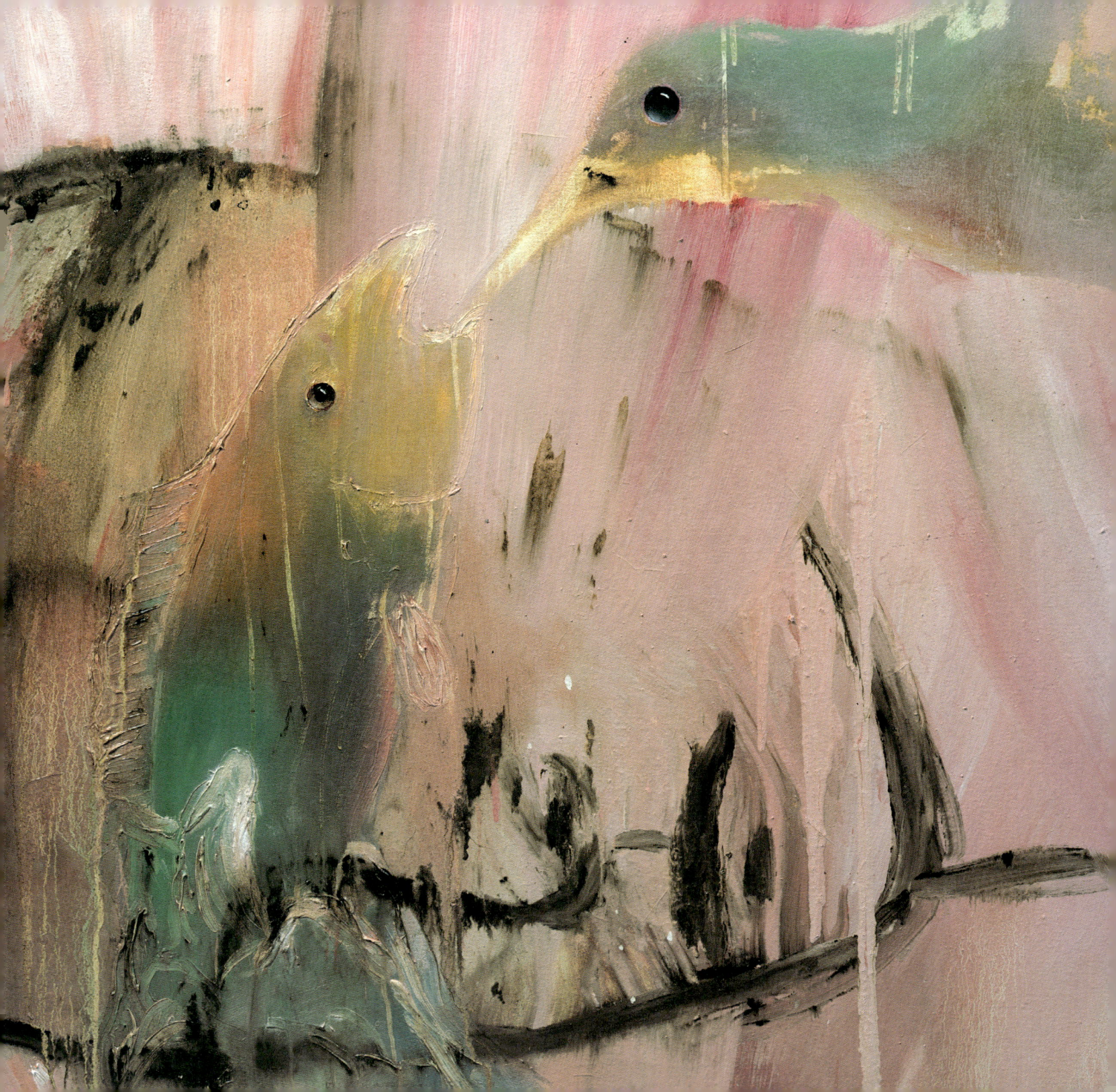

UNBROKEN POETRY

THE WORK OF ENRIQUE MARTINEZ CELAYA

ANNE TRUEBLOOD BRODZKY

with conversations between
Enrique Martínez Celaya, Amnon Yariv
and Donald Baechler

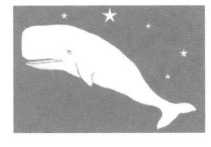

WHALE AND STAR
PRESS

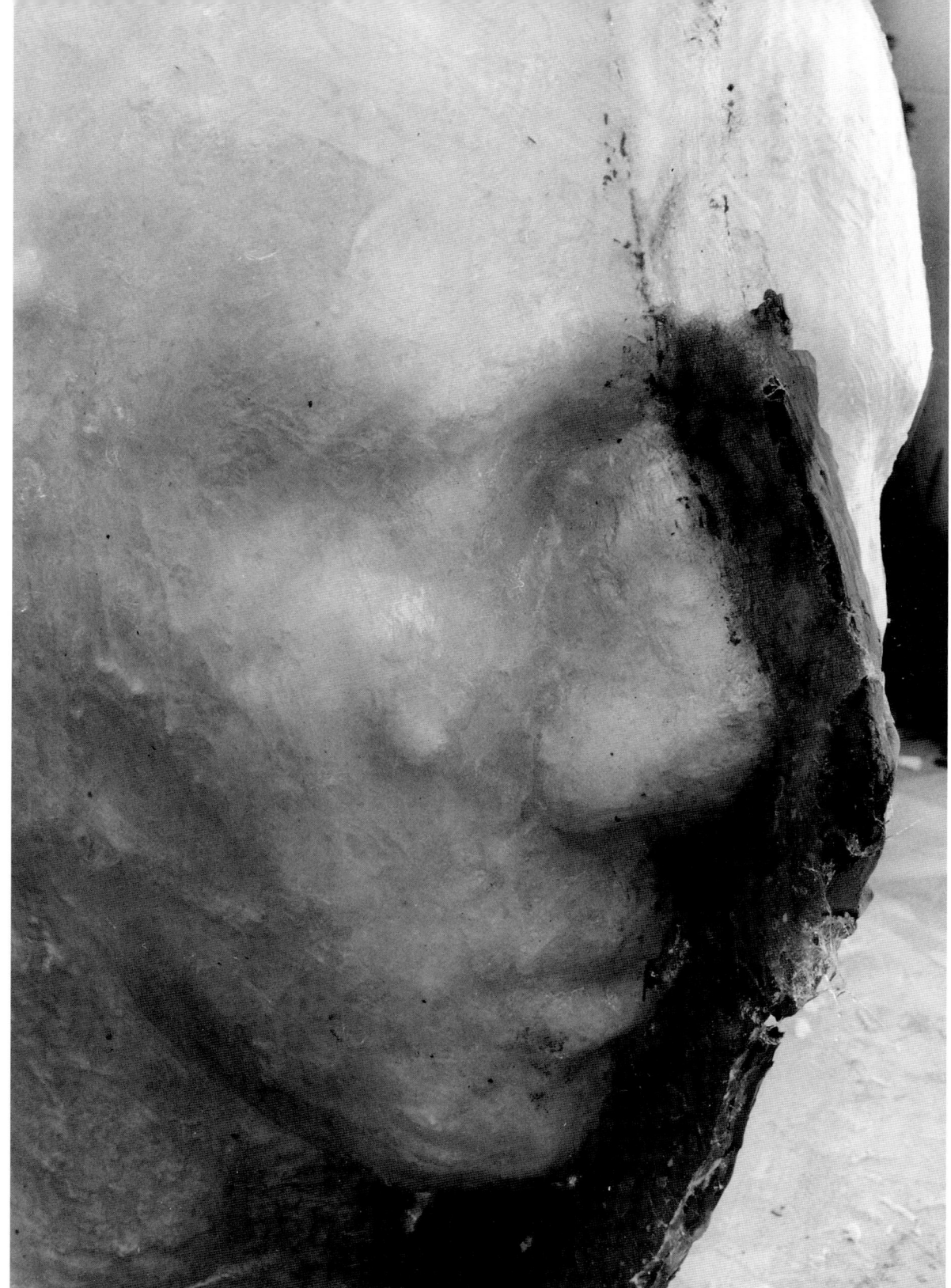

CONTENTS

Unbroken Poetry   9
   Anne Trueblood Brodzky

Compassion and Subjectivity   67
   Conversation with
   Amnon Yariv

Imagery and Process   78
   Conversation with
   Donald Baechler

List of Works   90

Chronology/Bibliography   93

Acknowledgments, Credits and Colophon   110

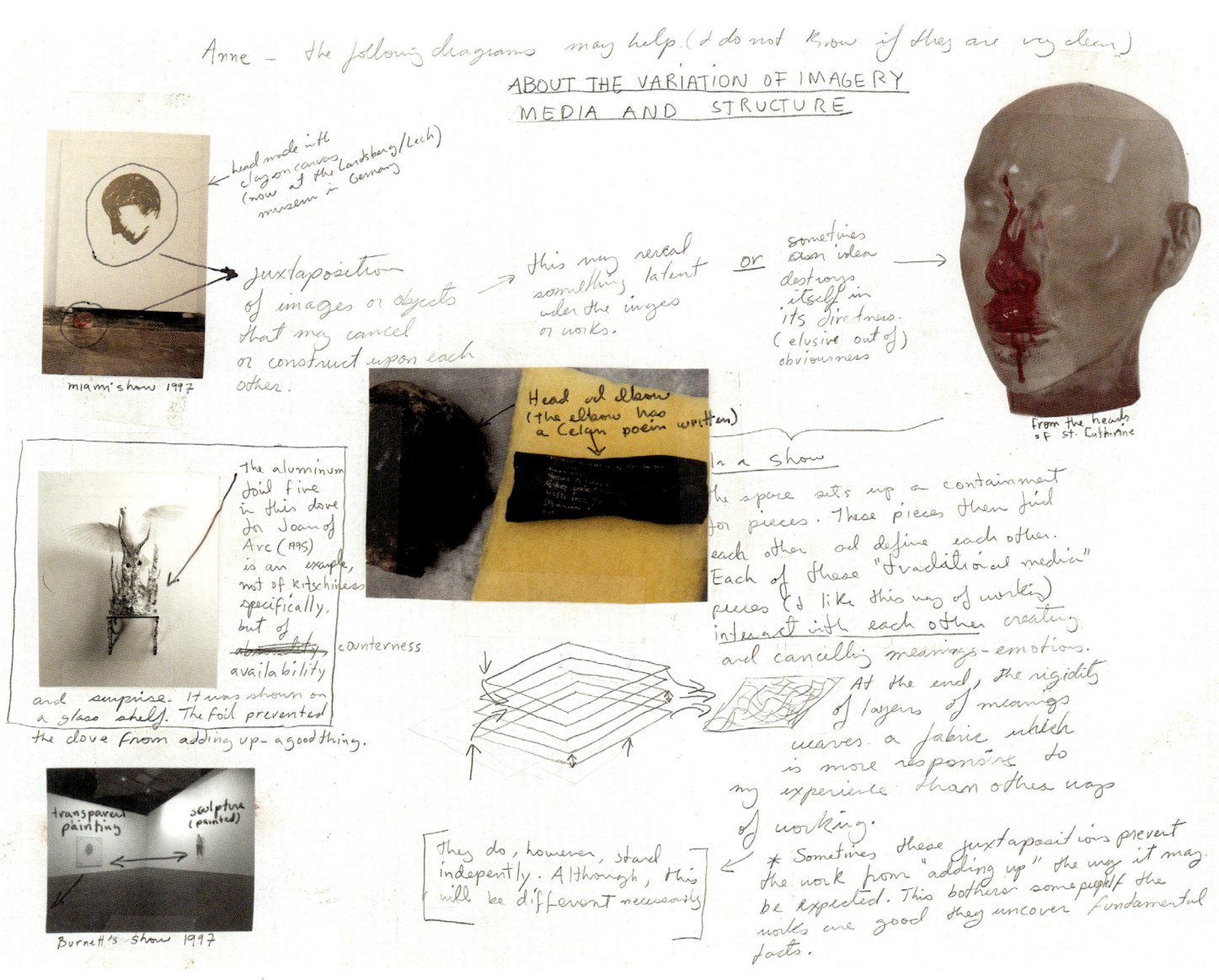

Anne — the following diagrams may help. (I do not know if they are very clear)

ABOUT THE VARIATION OF IMAGERY
MEDIA AND STRUCTURE

← head made with clay on canvas (now at the Landsberg/Lech museum in Germany)

Juxtaposition of images or objects that may cancel or construct upon each other.

this may reveal something latent under the images or works.

or sometimes even an idea destroys itself in its directness. (elusive out of) obviousness

from the heads of St. Catherine

miami show 1997

Head on elbow (the elbow has a Celan poem written)

the aluminum foil fire in this dove for Joan of Arc (1995) is an example, not of kitschiness specifically but of ~~obviousness~~ counterness availability

and surprise. It was shown on a glass shelf. The foil prevented the dove from adding up — a good thing.

In a show the space sets up a containment for pieces. These pieces then find each other and define each other. Each of these "traditional media" pieces (I like this way of working) interact with each other creating and cancelling meanings — emotions.

At the end, the rigidity of layers of meanings weaves a fabric which is more responsive to my experience than other ways of working.

transparent painting   sculpture (painted)

Burnett's show 1997

They do, however, stand independently. Although, this will be different necessarily

* Sometimes these juxtapositions prevent the work from "adding up" the way it may be expected. This bothers some people. If the works are good they uncover fundamental facts.

Notes by Enrique Martínez Celaya sent to the author in April 1999.

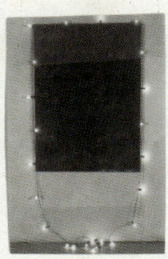

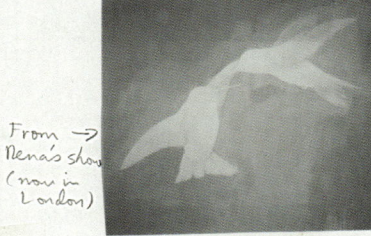

This x-mas lights
were a lesson in
the integrity of the
wall and the object
in relation to it.
the lights are immediate
shrine. These came from
no art (No Bottarelli etc)
came from coffee shop
in Puerto Rico.

From →
Nena's show
(now in
London)

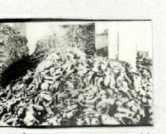

shoes in concentration
camp

→ In the new works
(as in all the others)
there is imagery that
should be understood
to be surrogates (Donald's word)
of the figure and the spirit.
These works are not about
birds, or heads or flowers.
Maybe this is true of
many works. All these
things are excuses, vehicles
to get at specific moments.
that exists as artworks but
that point beyond the
            artworks.

You asked me what I
was ~~thinking~~ about

- Melville
- loss and one's terms in acceptance of it
- artwork and its dismemberment.
- the past - me as counter
        └→ the objectivity of this count?

- Giorgione and Leonardo

- Is there a system that unifies
1) precision and imprecision (wittgenstein?)
2) Fragilities and strengths (Jung?)
3) Grace and horror (Leonardo)

— o —
What things are and what things
mean is what I think about
when I work. It makes the work
hard, it forces me to edit a lot and it
often leaves me with work that
I never set out to do.

I understand the problems of meaning.
The burden of action with this awareness
is what gives the work its charge.

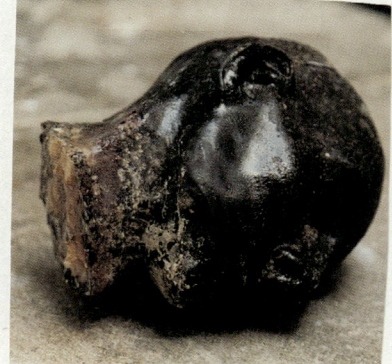

Head of resin, dirt and flowers
from "Berlin". Tom has this
head now.

A NOTE:

1. Most art works are not ambitious enough.
2. Most audiences are seemingly satisfied with that.
   a) Comfort with diminished expectations is intellectually sleek.
3. Intellectual sleekness ≠ sophistication.
4. Intellectual sleekness ⇒ facile.
5. Art is a market of supply and demand.
6. Demand is always for signifiers of arrival — comfort in ones position.
7. The victorians had repressed desires take the form of allegory and myth.
8. This time now has repressed fears take the form of fantasies of refinement.
9. The clothes are here, there is just no emperor

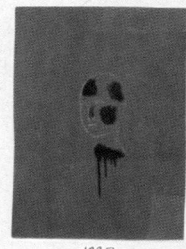
1997
the secrets

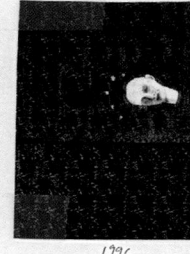
1996
Saint Cat. Orleans

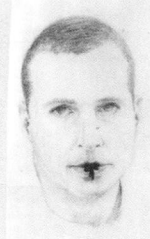
1996
Self Portrait

— It is this kind of work that makes some dismiss it as if they knew it. "Catholic, sentimental, a known figurative narrative."
I think that my work has all the trappings to be misread. It is a complicated reconciliation. Nothing for me to do here. Maybe this book?

If a head has roses inbeded in the resin at the discontinuity (or cut), of course, I see the desire for romance in their interpretation. For me, Julio Galan or Richard Serra are romantics. This work of mine is something else. Horror & Beauty are neither courted nor denied. Those two positions are my idea of romantics.

When I use "romantic" I try to mean what I think people mean. It has no relationship to the great romantic "movement". A great and misunderstood period.

UNBROKEN POETRY
ANNE TRUEBLOOD BRODZKY

We are in the presence of an artist whose project is no less than the distillation of memory from intensely observed fragments, both painful and pleasurable. Enrique Martínez Celaya takes loss and its transcendence through consciousness as the pervasive theme in his painting, drawing, sculpture, photography, and poetry. Loss is transcended by an accumulation of imagery and matrix that functions like the "unbroken poetry" he finds in the whole of Melville's *Moby Dick*. The artist is not narrator. He does not relate his theme; yet it is all-pervasive. One sees constantly the struggle between paired ideas of beauty and aridity, or triads of violence and tenderness and distance.

He works—not abstractly but with concrete imagery, often using sharply contrasting images and textures—with seeming opposites. His is a world where hummingbirds feed fish and a tulip's flesh-like petal caresses a truncated human head; a world where torn or slashed canvas is sewn again, beribboned; a world of dryness and implied moisture.

Martínez Celaya's Cuban roots, Spanish and Puerto Rican experience, his New York and California education in

9

Physics and Art, as well as his accomplishments, both academic and artistic, speak of one simultaneously at home, yet homeless in the world. "His is the art of what remains. Wisp is powerful; faint scent of everything wafted on indifferent wind. If something is erased it has been. If it is forgotten or remembered, it has existed." [Carl Heyward, ms. 1999.]

Nothing is quick about the making, the meaning, or the cumulative effect of the paintings, drawings, and poems of Martínez Celaya. In the words of William Butler Yeats, "peace comes dropping slow," in the distilling of one's perception of this artist's closely interrelated works whose layerings, concealments, revelations, and clustered images are compressed, filtered gradually from his memory. Memory, and the artist's fierce desire to capture and reconcile it in imagery of water, blood, nectar, tears, mazes, flowers, birds, fish, and the fragmented human body, is the central theme. Memory and the related issues of loss, pain, privacy, and the boon of consciousness are explored throughout these works.

I will deal briefly with some of the means at the command of Martínez Celaya which may draw him into our ken as an artist and poet. We will then look at his themes and ways of working to illumine some of his process and its prevailing continuity of concern. Among the experiential forces that Martínez Celaya draws upon are his sense of exile or foreignness which he first became aware of as an acutely intelligent young child; his deep knowledge and love of literature; his disciplined experience as a physicist; and his rigorous training in art.

Who is this artist who had, at the young age of 30, already produced constellations of disturbing and ambitious works? I first met Enrique Martínez Celaya in his small, San Francisco

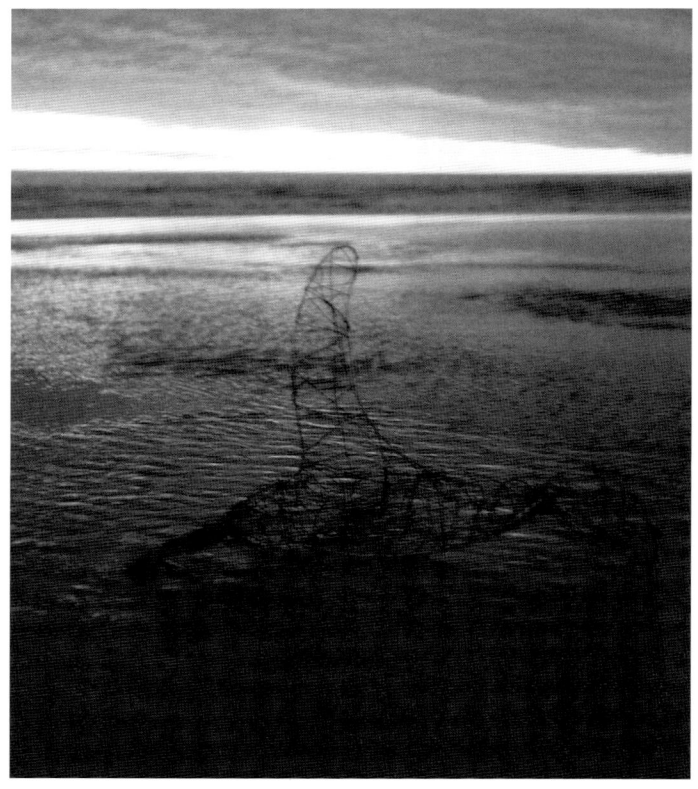

Armature for sculpture, Venice, 1999

The Trouble with Memory 1993 ▶

studio in 1989, just after he had made the momentous decision to relinquish a successful career in the field of quantum physics and devote himself full time to his art. He was already an accomplished painter of arresting figurative work. Martínez Celaya is an artist who is radically concerned with meaning, choosing "traditional" modes of art making (drawing, oil painting, carving, and sculpture) and yet placing his works in conceptual arrangements with the keenest of poetic imaginations. Radically, at a time when much in the current art world is banal, this artist desires that the families of seemingly dissimilar works that make up this collection be received as the poetically unified works that they are.

A childhood and youth uprooted from his native Cuba— moving to Madrid, to Puerto Rico, and then to New York—fragments and seasons with sharp loss his early memories. Perhaps these nomadic years deprived an acutely aware child of the solace that George Eliot mentions:

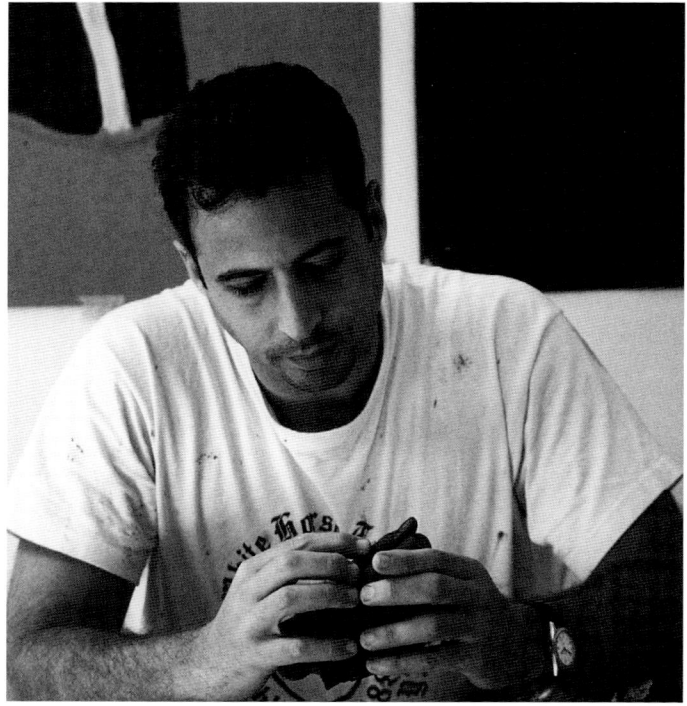

"A human life, I think, should be well rooted in some spot of the native land where it may get the love of tender kinship for the face of the earth, for whatever will give that early home a familiar unmistakable difference amid the future widening of knowledge. But this blessed persistence in which affection can take place ... was missing..."

[*Daniel Deronda,* 1876]

Born in Cuba in 1964, Martínez Celaya has recollections of his grandfather feeding his birds across an open courtyard: "To me there is a truth in him performing that act. Fixed in time is how the bird looked with the light hitting its feathers and the wrinkled hand reaching out." The intensity of this fragment of numinous imagery and

Martínez Celaya's habit of *trusting* it to stand in for a whole cluster of meanings becomes clear as one examines his works.

At the age of eight, the child emigrated with his mother and younger brother to Madrid to join his father. Each time he left a place, he would try fervently to fix in his conscious mind certain smells and sights as a stay against the anticipated loss and chaos of forgetting, a stay against the obliteration of the familiar. Walt Whitman might have described the particular fixed intensity of that child when he wrote:

> "There was a child went forth every day;
> And the first object he looked upon
> that object he became;
> And that object became part of him for
> the day, or a certain part of the day, or for many
> years, or stretching cycles of years." [1855]

Whitman's evocation of that rare capacity that allows such acuity parallels Martínez Celaya's ability to recall fragmented images.

Recognizing that their son had a gift for drawing and that he longed to be able to render well, his parents apprenticed him at age eleven to painter Bartoldo Mayol. Mayol instilled in him his own great love for the process of making art. As one biographer said of Leonardo da Vinci, "what he saw, he drew." And as his paintings evidence, Martínez Celaya was also an avid drawer. Growing up, he had little formal knowledge of art or of art history, though from an early age, he saw and loved Leonardo "as an entity, not just as an artist," and for the example that Leonardo's life offers. It was not until the artist was seventeen and studying at Cornell that he visited the Museum of Modern

Mayol had certain similarities to my father... a certain fancifulness. He walked with a cane and a hat. He lived in a Spanish time that no longer existed, something about his whole behavior did not fit the context of where he was. And yet it was perfect for him. He was not a very successful artist, even by Puerto Rican standards, but he loved art. When he was drawing he would surrender to it, he was still enamored with making something appear out of nothing, like somebody who learns to draw for the first time. There was a lot of tenderness in him, and tenderness toward his work. To see his love for the work was the greatest lesson I learned during my time with him. I know many successful artists, many of whom do it just as an occupation. They will never understand it. I think this is what I got from him.

He was very disciplined and inspiring as a teacher. He appreciated rigorous work. My parents wanted me to be able to do something on Saturdays and I painted and drew constantly. I kept books of my drawings and I did many pastels and oils on paper. I bought a color-by-numbers set and then I just used the oils to paint things I liked. I wasn't good at going by the numbers. My pieces and the work helped me with some issues that were going on in my life. I never thought of the larger enterprise of art. I just wanted to be able to render very well; that was my idea of what good art was. I don't think I saw much of art at all. I knew Velazquez and Goya. And Leonardo, whom I loved. I was uninformed about modern art for most of my teenage years. [†]

[†]*Unless otherwise stated, all quotes are from a series of interviews between Martínez Celaya and Brodzky in April 1999.*

Art in New York and saw his first piece of 20th Century art, Picasso's *Les Demoiselles d'Avignon* (1907). Suddenly, and with that painting in particular, he discovered the wider world of art. A part of what the young Martínez Celaya was responding to then is still visible in his own work now. Picasso, as John Richardson points out

> "addresses in the *Demoiselles*, notably...[Baudelaire's] adulation of what he called 'pure art... the type of beauty peculiar to evil, the beauty in the horrible' or his notion of whoredom as an ideal subject for an artist."

[*A Life of Picasso: 1907-1917*, p. 14.]

Upon his distinguished graduation from Cornell and his entry into the Ph.D. program in physics at Berkeley, Martínez Celaya made the striking discovery that he could no longer do art on the side. From that moment on— through graduate art programs at Berkeley and at the University of California at Santa Barbara, where he won highest honors in art—his career as an artist rose. Like the young Arshile Gorky, Martínez Celaya ran through the major art movements of the first half of this century. In 1994, before a summer in Skowhegan where he was to meet Donald Baechler and Allen Ginsberg, the artist found himself deeply involved with his earliest series of black paintings. Now he began the ferocious ongoing dialogue with the theme that is central to his work: loss and transcendence in the struggle against forgetfulness.

Today, in Martinez Celaya's studio, one can hear the sound of water bubbling through a blue-tiled fountain he has built, as it is filtered through the open grill work of an antique set of immense, hand-carved wooden shutters

Picasso's eyes, the aspect of his gaze, cut through reality. In the tug of war between the beauty of his pieces and their violence and destruction is where the emotional power comes in. It is the late Picassos that I like most for their confidence in the paint. They are earthly bound, powerful, with unrelenting toughness, even when they are delicate.

•••

My father, Marcos, also paints. He paints with great belief in the power of painting and with love for the objects and subjects that he renders. The results are wonderful naïve works that are very convincing of their need to exist, which is something that can not be said of most work today. He is currently painting three large paintings in his church.

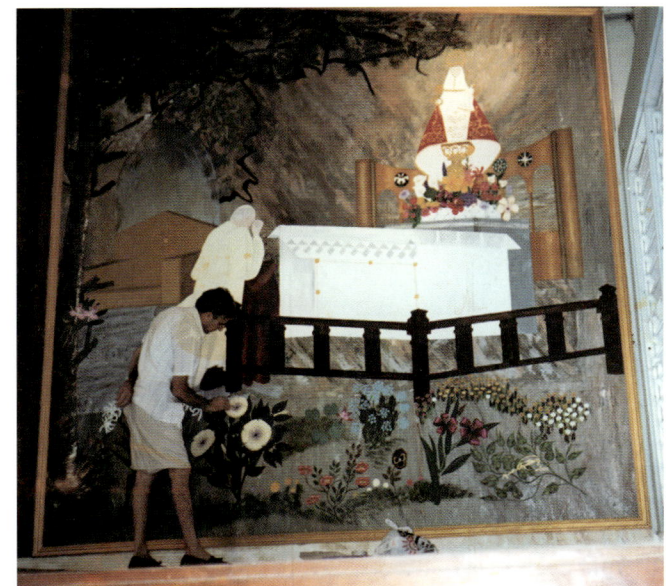

Marcos Martínez painting in the church of Nuestra Sra. de Covadonga, 1998

No Doubt Good Writing 1995

from India. One enters the studio through vast, high, adamantine, rusted steel doors also made by the artist.

The contrasting closures and openings, the sounds and stillness, all contribute to the intensity of this private sanctuary. This studio, reminiscent of the home and garden in Cuba of the artist's Spanish grandfather, was the setting in which I viewed Martinez Celaya's recent works. Surely this place has given birth to some of the most difficult, metaphysical paintings and drawings that I have seen.

It is in Martínez Celaya's first black paintings, like *The Trouble with Memory* (p. 11), *Three Wounds*, or the affecting work on paper called *No Doubt Good Writing* (p. 15*)*, that one sees him initially "put together the idea of referential anecdotal implication within the work where the sheer presence and physical quality of the work become important." It is here, too, that Martínez Celaya's preoccupation with obliterating and obscuring words or images began to take shape. This impulse to hide the content of his works, he believes, is related to an "aspect of privacy."

The artist's sketchbooks—he has filled approximately two each year since 1991—are crucial in coming to a fuller understanding of his creative process. In flipping through these pages, one will occasionally come across a pregnant poetic visual image such as *white island black sea* (p. 85). Elsewhere a passage will reveal a profoundly predictive direction in his work such as the 1993 "notes on black."

Each sketchbook also functions as a diary, storybook, and map of the artist's inspiration. There are places where, already deeply engaged in a painting, he breaks off and turns to his sketchbook to record a poem inspired by the painting. Similarly, a drawn or written image in a poem is

In some ways, my work has always tried to undermine what is created, so there is a constant battle for the elimination of the work itself, a struggle against its full survival. In *No Doubt Good Writing*, I could not live with what I had written but I could live with the writing denied.

These "notes on black" appear as an entry in Martínez Celaya's sketchbook for January 24, 1993:

...most of all the wonder of wonders. Black. Totally alive and vital these black paintings call me. They call me to do black. They call me to do thickness of darkness. Blackness, prayer of silence. Maybe I have just begun to understand the black paintings...every other color seems subordinated (except perhaps white and red). To make paintings that are mysterious, more silent, yet more powerful. Go further into the poetry of feelings. Austere and contemplative. I want to find a way to make them breathe.

gates	solitude
blues	unheard cries
night	comfort of being
wind	magic alchemy

sometimes the primary source for what will later appear in his paintings. Images such as the disembodied head on its side in *Right Word* (p. 18), and the schematic visualizations of cuts, wounds, and tears which appear sewn, bound, and repaired in part in the white on white work of 1996, *The Liar and The Thief* (p. 19) originated in sketchbooks. The sketchbooks, which become increasingly textual over the years, are also mined as sources for titles of visual works. Occasionally they offer elaborate schematic diagrams (pp. 6-8).

It is about this time, also, that one begins to see the densely layered surfaces of these works begin more and more to be gashed and then restitched, and oftentimes beribboned in imitation of the very process of repairing or revising memory, of shoring up forgetfulness.

Images of the head are central to the work of Martínez Celaya, in all his chosen media, since their first appearance in paint in 1995 and their somewhat earlier arrival in a sketchbook. I would like to look at this crucial image because it so strenuously relates to his dominant theme of loss, consciousness, and ultimately, transcendence.

"Heads," the artist commented, "are the armatures of memories." As containers, they are sometimes all that is left of a memory. This idea is suggestive of the ancient Arctic Inuit conviction that the skeletal head and bones are the repository for the spirit, that which remains. The dismembered head and some of the body parts he uses also act as metaphors for moments.

In his constellations of works, *Joan of Arc* and *St. Catherine* (p. 40), meaning inheres in each portion of an environmental piece. Heads of the saints become vehicles or metaphors for what their life and experience was about.

In *The Liar and The Thief* the painting is the object, and it can suffer cuts, it can suffer attacks, and you can mend it. This aspect of tearing and working with this surface as if it did not have integrity any more, that it was corrupted somehow, was an important thing to me and it still is. But the desire was not to make the wounds for their own sake, or to romanticize the idea of wounding as a metaphor.

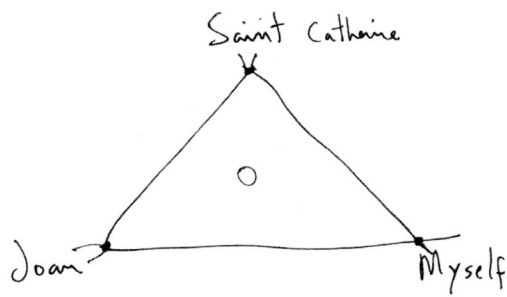

Unless otherwise stated, all sketches and diagrams are from the sketchbooks of Enrique Martínez Celaya.

The Right Word 1995

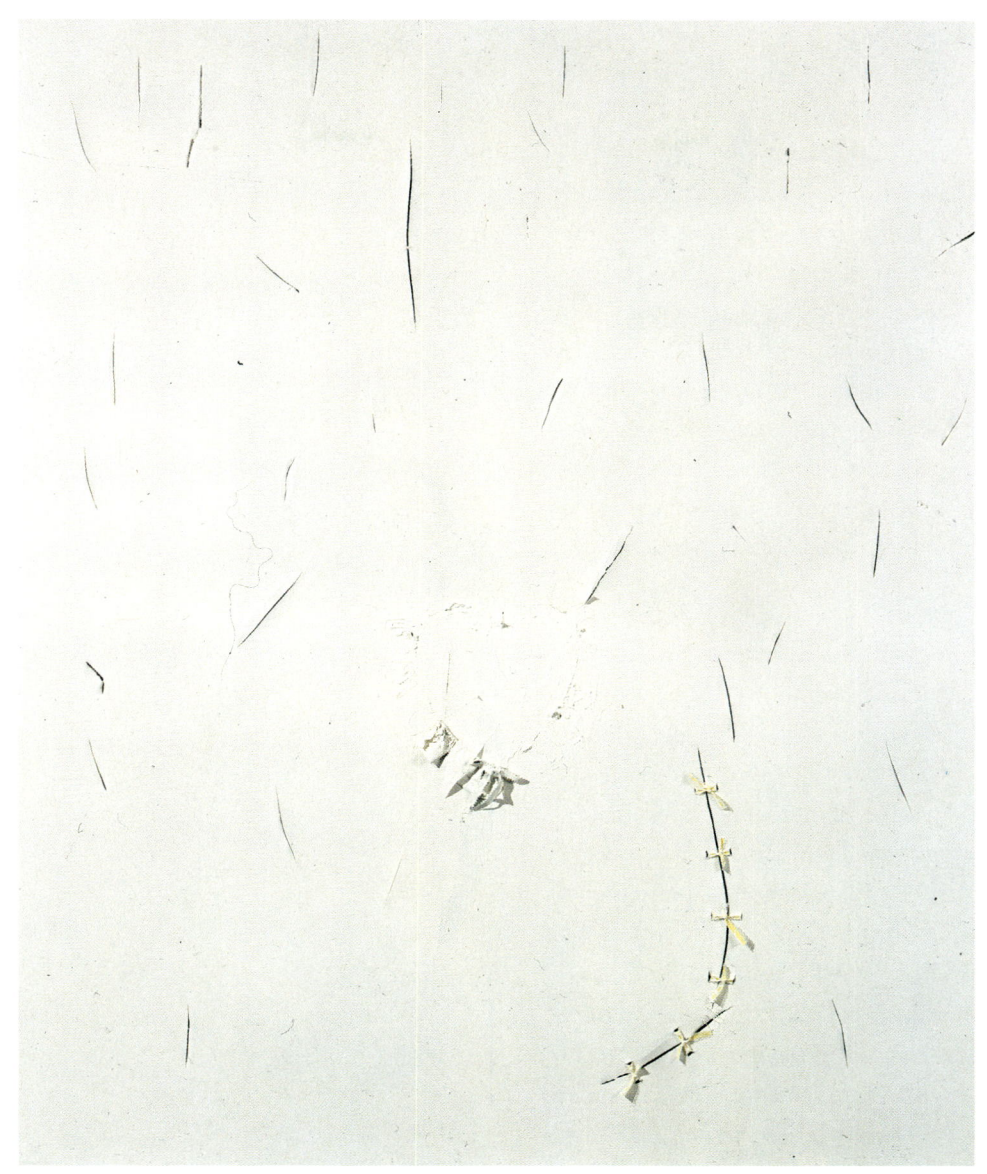

The Liar and the Thief 1996

In the paintings and drawings such as *Head with Lilies* or *A Neck in Ashes* (p. 46), and in the monumental disembodied sculpted heads that rest on pillows on the floor or on pedestals, one can begin to approach the complexity of method with which the artist builds his environments. In the elaborately redolent paintings of 1998 and 1999, the head takes on yet more layers of meaning. As the artist makes clear in the passage to the right, the meaning of the head expands to include consciousness itself. With these works Martínez Celaya also abjures painting as theatre, which he believes the use of the body fragment prevents. He selects instead the more comprehensive, active arena in which transformation of meaning and function can occur within the work itself, without reference to narrative.

Heads are of great importance as emblems of sorrow, as seen in the artist's photograph of the covered head of the sorrowing woman, *Size of a Wound* (p. 89). The sense of her loss is ratcheted up to such a degree of intensity that it is nearly unbearable. In the body of Martínez Celaya's works, as in this photograph of a fabric-veiled, sculpted head, the covering, taping, bandaging, or layering over of a wound or of a potentially erotic passage or an obscured text, renders the same emotional compression. It is a vomiting head in the work *News of My Virtue*, that performs a pivotal role in his major multiple object installation piece, *Works of Loss, Renouncement and Redemption* [Burnett Miller, 1997]. As the artist points out, to vomit is to commit an aspect of purging. In a central way, the vomiting head ties up the whole narrative of covering and purging.

In later works such as the two 9' x 10' *Quiet Night* pieces (p.44-45), and *Open Sky the Feeder* (p.61) the head with its pregnant roundness is the site of both wounding and

Are the heads self-portraits? Well, I think that in the work there are always coverings, stand-ins, and revelations. I think it is always my head, but it's my head as thought, or my head as remembered. It's not that important whether or not it looks like me. As a matter of fact, often when it looks like me I will change it. Some things have vestiges of self-portraiture. It's like the way a mirror works. I am purposely trying to distance them from me so I can see them.

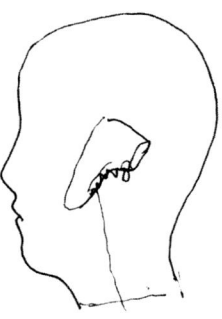

blue - baby shoe

healing. The head as an object, becomes a reliquary for extreme sorrow, a locus for bleeding wounds whose suppurating red moisture attracts, as to red nectar, the hummingbird, a violent aggressor.

In 1995, the concept of a simultaneity of works in different media that speak to each other, and that depend on each other to create an environment, emerged with the *Joan of Arc* show. In the exhibition the artist thought about space and how it could be fractured by introducing seemingly disparate elements. This was most successfully executed in *Loss, Renouncement and Redemption*, an environmental work where one finds an early and prime example of the way in which there are collisions between loss and transcendence and the ways in which individual works are related: all speak simultaneously, all depend on one another. *Loss, Renouncement and Redemption* was installed in a large space. The ensemble included a piece entitled *The River* (p. 23), a life-sized sculpture of a young woman, painted with a blue sky from head to waist, which hung on the wall 12 feet above the floor. A landscape was painted on her waist and, from waist to feet, a river. Her stomach had been opened, filled with flowers, and resewn. Across from it was a transparent piece called *The Burden of Your Hand* (p.27), based on a poem of the same title, in which a silver hand hung down amidst translucent layers of stretched, white chiffon. The work's stretchers could be seen through the material and formed a frame. Sixteen tiny paintings of dead hummingbirds on 8" x 8" linen squares formed a poignant line. A large white painting with a small vomiting head was on the fourth wall, and as one entered, there was a large piece with a tiny intense landscape called *Deep Water*. Martínez Celaya saw the works as a meta-narrative like the stations of the cross;

The question of where does the consciousness or the spirit lie is, of course, a very, very old question. In some ways, at least tangentially, it is involved in this work. I try to understand why the birds and all these other images came into my work. I think they came in because I didn't want to make figure paintings. This is part of the dismemberment aspect; when you have a full figure in a painting it somehow forces the painting to become something of a theatre. I think that when you look at a painting with a figure, you look at the figure and you empathize with the figure like it was an actor on a stage. You feel through the actor some larger message. A painting is always somewhat like a stage, somewhat an intermediary. I wanted to be as direct as possible. The formal constraints that I impose in my work, allow me to then hold things in place. Relying on the rigidity of these choices, you can then take some liberties with what you can do in the painting.

independent but thematically bound. There was no clear relationship between the aesthetic look of the pieces, yet they formed a coherent whole.

I believe that when Martínez Celaya deals with water—whether it be a river, a lake, or a pond of still water like that in his lyrical, erotic work called *First War* (p.42)—he invests water with the quiet meaning that Melville writes of when he says at the beginning of *Moby Dick* that "water and meditation are forever wedded."

Consider now Martínez Celaya's process in the reconciliation of seeming opposites in his work over the last three years. It is clear that he is preoccupied with meaning, with contraries. Martínez Celaya speaks of his interest in "the force of interaction between two parts that generates a third part, [that makes] the true part." And he talks of an "aspect of consciousness that is born to this friction between two parts. As is frequently the case with Leonardo da Vinci, horror has been distilled in such a way as to generate a flower of beauty out of it." In recent work, marked examples of three kinds of transformation can be found in *Acceptance of Longing* (pp. 33, 80) and *Tu Brazo* (p. 34).

The prone hummingbirds in the former two pieces with their apparent union of longing and satiety suggest a state of sleep or death. In *Tu Brazo*, the severed arm is lifted, blessed, even born aloft by tulips that resemble wings. These works, with their soft, warm, brown monochrome or silvered grounds and their relatively minimal expressiveness, take the states of passionate longing and pain and the desuetude of a severed arm, no longer able to function and provide, through a transference of poetic functions: the ability to rest, to act, to make something of beauty.

These "pairs" appear as an entry in Martínez Celaya's sketchbook for April 8, 1991:

aridness	beauty
violence	tenderness
nearness	distance
chaos	order/belief
obliterate	reveal
conceal	open
dismember	make whole
dissolve	coalesce
wound	heal/mend/protect
hunger	satiety
dry	wet
horror	beauty

The River 1997 ▶

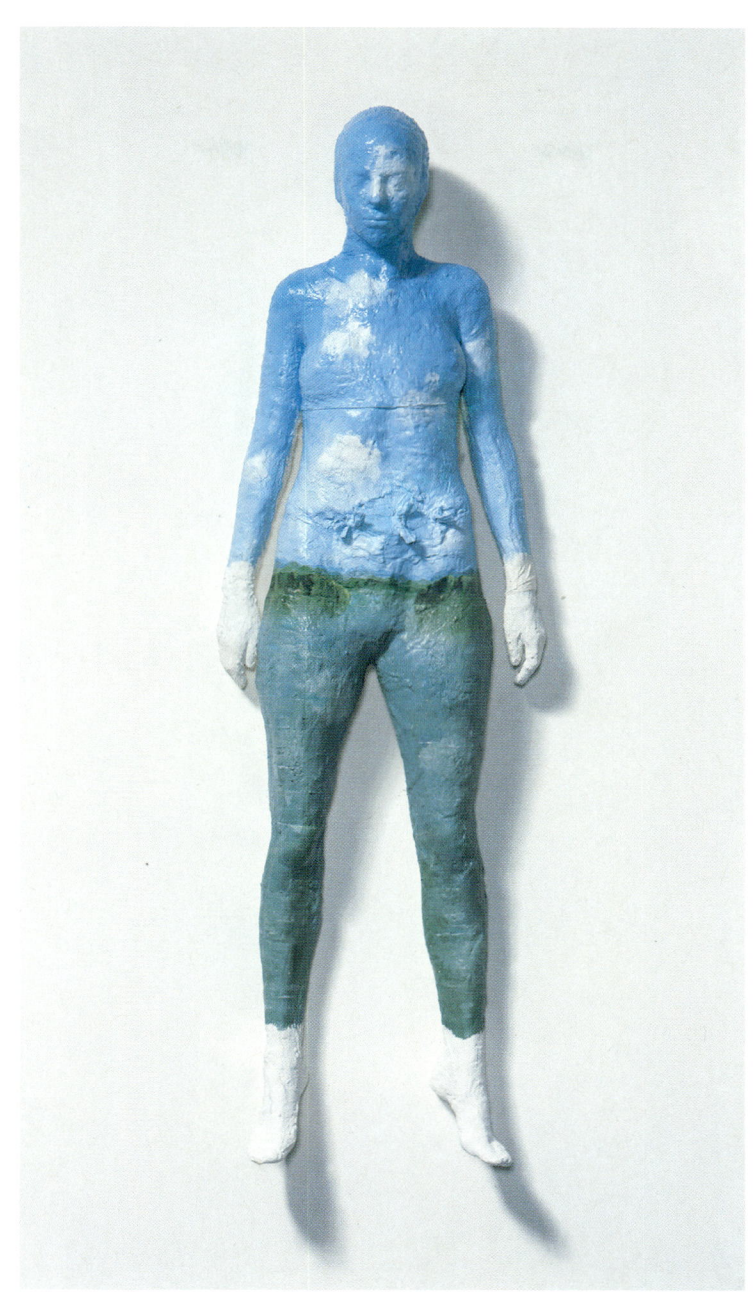

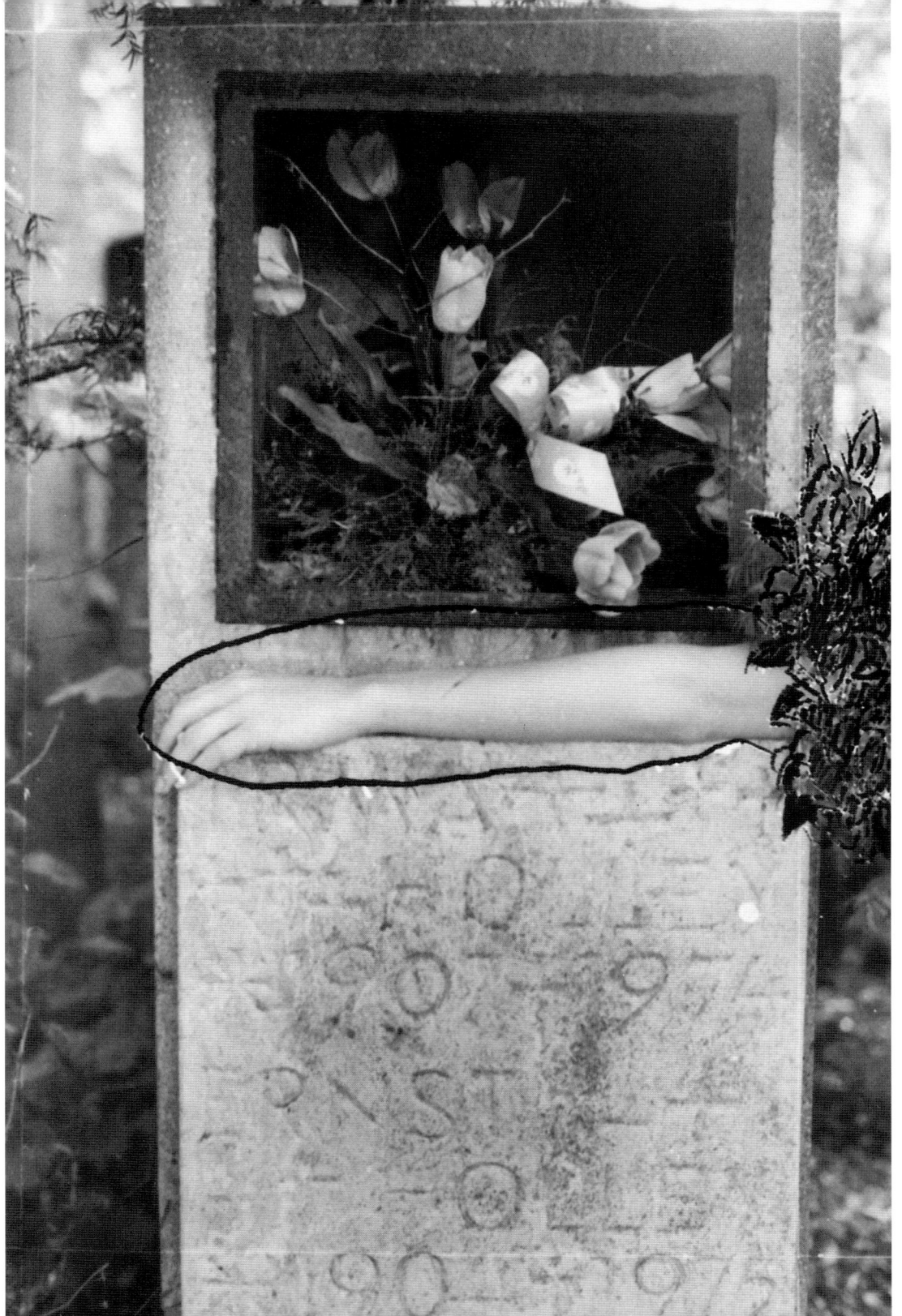

The imagery in the works of 1998 and 1999 is limited to hummingbirds, swans, parts of the body, rose petals, tulips, and fish. Its surfaces are often suffused with a rosy color. Other times they are dark and richly tactile with distressed grounds composed of tar and oil over wax. Even when the surface is sandy colored and scumbled with the remains of rubbed out messages, the effect is less austere, less minimal. In this work the confluence of ideas of loss and transcendence is palpable. Now one truly witnesses the mysteries of becoming. The canvas or other support (it might be paper or velvet or an old, translucent lace-edged tablecloth) and the action (a hummingbird trying to feed four leaping fish or a black swan dissolving into a loosely painted, rose shaped maze) join in syncretic union.

It is this near magic joining of opposites, not by any simplistic black and white ambiguous embrace, but through the poetic alembic of Martínez Celaya's fusion, which renders these art works massively powerful. They pull you through their experience of union.

The lessons Martínez Celaya is learning from Herman Melville reinforce what he has already attempted to do in his work. Reading Melville has encouraged him to be perhaps more outrageous, in layering meanings. These risks can be seen in the shocking scale of paintings in which hummingbirds and swans nearly fill the picture plane, and in the way a vast rose petal dwarfs the drawn image of the small metal bed in the Joan of Arc installation piece. In this painting one sees the poetic fusion of discordant elements created by an artist passionately engaged with syncretic action and reconciliation. When he spoke of *Moby Dick* as a work of unbroken poetry he was referring

◀ Winter and silk flowers (detail) 1998

... I remember the look and feel of things and I remember minute components of memories which make perfect sources for paintings because they are disconnected from larger things: the smell of somebody cooking, a particular living room, a certain age. They are very hard to explain well with words but they translate into painting more easily. The past is present like a mystery that you try to solve for all time.

•••

If you look at a photograph of something, and you try to understand everything that is involved in the image the subject will remain elusive. [Some memories] do not present themselves easily as answers. There's no specific answer to understand. Say, my grandfather coming out of his dental office and sitting down and rocking in the chair in a dark room.; there's no answer that you can provide, because you don't know what the question is. But obviously something meaningful is there, and because one cannot formalize a question very easily, it's very difficult to formalize the answer. I think paintings try to capture some of those elusive feelings that flutter around and then reinvest them again with spirit.

also to Melville's use of metaphor to join memory with consciousness and wholeness, an ambition that Martínez Celaya is striving for in this and future works. He is nourished by Melville's juxtaposition of equilibrium and clarity with loss and forgetting and believes that Melville provides a skeleton, a sort of foundation for what he is trying to do.

As part of his practiced way of working, Martínez Celaya takes his confidence as painter and poet back into his own past and forward into his avid interest in encountering and coming to poetic terms with a new city, a new terrain. Thus memory, often fractured memory, is the stuff of his work. I am thinking now of his long poem, *Berlin*, and his new unpublished poem, *My Father* (1997), which, as several of his poems have, appeared written on a gallery wall, holding equal pride of place with a sculpture piece or a large work on paper. Fragmented memories create perhaps a predilection for fragmented imagery. It is clear that Martínez Celaya's way of working as painter or sculptor is like that of a wordsmith. In a remarkably strong and fragile piece called *The Poet*, he first uses a disembodied arm, the beginning of the disembodied figure. It is a small arm, white against a loose grid of thickly piled silver leaf on a canvas of five feet by six feet. The artist's interest in this image grew, in part, out of his fascination with paintings that push the limit of figuration to the point of being almost entirely abstract.

In many of the artist's pieces there are elements of cloth that will tie, bandages that will wrap, tape that will fix. It seems to me that beyond the symbolic aspects of concealing and revealing there is also, in the work, a strong motif or element of wanting to heal or protect.

In a formal sense, the large *Untitled, Wound* (1997), comments in a very powerful way on this desire to join the

When I first arrived in Spain I remember the smell of fruits coming through the airplane door. For some reason Spain smelled like fruit. In Spain I became familiar with not belonging somewhere. That was a feeling I had not known before. Then I became practiced at being a foreigner. There are a lot of feelings related to that. Only now do I understand how I was confused for all those years. I thought I wasn't, but I was very confused.

•••

The first arm is an arm without a hand. I wanted to get closer to the idea of the poet, for there is a certain amount of futility in artwork in general and in poetry in particular. Incomplete, the arm becomes potential... possibility... if I only had a hand... Months later I created a poem and a new transparent piece called *The Burden of Your Hand* in which we see the hand that disappeared.

The Burden of Your Hand 1997 ▶
Collection of the Progressive Corporation, Cleveland

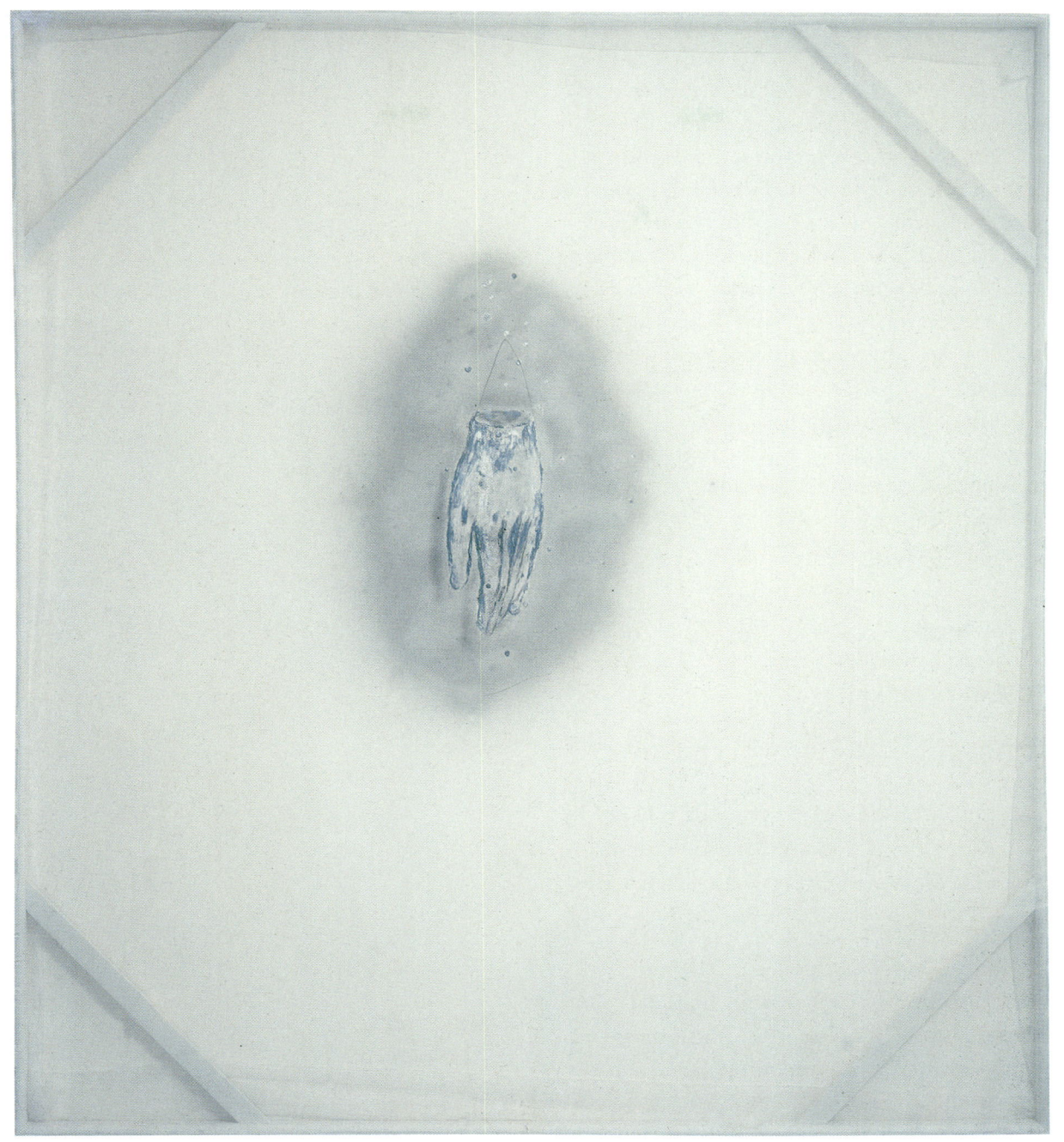

violent with the tender in simultaneous healing. Here oil on crimson flocked velvet suggests the colors of blood holding at its calm center a vertical slit, delicately painted in white and rose madder. If the wound and the healing appear simultaneously here, the process is more subtly implied in such works as *A boy in his room* (p. 39), where a head is covered completely in cloth, and in certain nearly abstract white canvases in which layering reveals transparent leaching of color like that of crushed pomegranate seeds. In the piece called *Just Great*, with a constellation of pale pink stainings on a dry white ground, those who look closely find the drawn head of a bird in whose upraised beak appears the crudely lettered word, "untrue." Such implied woundings or healings suggest the poetic practice of Spanish poet Miguel Hernandez [d. 1942], whose tragic but light-filled poetry is close to Martínez Celaya's heart, and to his own mode of making:

> "The sky is losing blood
> lowly out of wounds.
> The green deepens the
> shadows under leaves."

[from *Still Fields*, translated by Timothy Baland]

Sometimes the support itself suggests comfort, as in one of a series of Martínez Celaya's works on soft white cotton quilting. On some of these works the image of a flowering head is applied.

One returns again to Melville as a force in Martínez Celaya's work. In Melville's *Moby Dick,* he finds the collision of clarity and equilibrium opposed with austerity and loss to be a fundamental inspiration for the work found in his own Venice studio.

Sometimes mending acknowledges the futility of trying to fix something. You work knowing it is a failing enterprise. That desire is apparent in the photographs of tombs in Berlin. The gestures of those who tried to stop the erosion of memory by creating statues are both tender and futile. I photographed this very physical thing to remember those who had been loved. I think it is like when somebody dies and the loved ones put make-up on that person to make him look nice. There's such tenderness in that futile gesture. And I'm interested in trying to heal and to patch and to mend things, even when it becomes absurd, even when it no longer makes sense.

The nature of memory, its distillation, becomes palpable in the work entitled *Feeder and Voice* (p. 31). Everything touched on thus far is epitomized in this single painting. For me this painting holds depths of metaphysical verity that require taking a retrospective look at Martínez Celaya's pervasive use of the hummingbird as a living metaphor for consciousness. The hummingbird, which first entered the artist's sketchbooks as early as 1993 and 1994 in tiny, quickly reiterated drawings, began to invade the vast, often arid surfaces of paintings on canvas and paper as tiny, vibrantly colored creatures or miniaturized lifeless ones, sometimes so small in scale as to be barely discerned.

Hummingbirds, with their near miraculous ability to hover in mid-air and ability to travel as far as 500 miles, have been viewed in many cultures in the Americas as tangible evidence of magic. They are of course also known for their aggressive behavior and, a few varieties, for their voices. For Martínez Celaya they have many layers of meaning.

In *Feeder and Voice*, three fish painted a dark iron red and one the color of old ivory leap out of densely textured shadows, their mouths open, to be fed by a hummingbird sketched in incredibly agile white lines as he tries to feed all four fish with his long beak. The surfaces are paper overlaid with wax and with luminous brown-black tar; the work is composed in four segments of square proportion.

For Martínez Celaya, the fish is a "very earthly thing bound in reality. It is very different than the way I think of the hummingbird."

In *Circumstance* (p. 97), two huge white hummingbirds nearly fill the pale, ivory hued picture plane with their

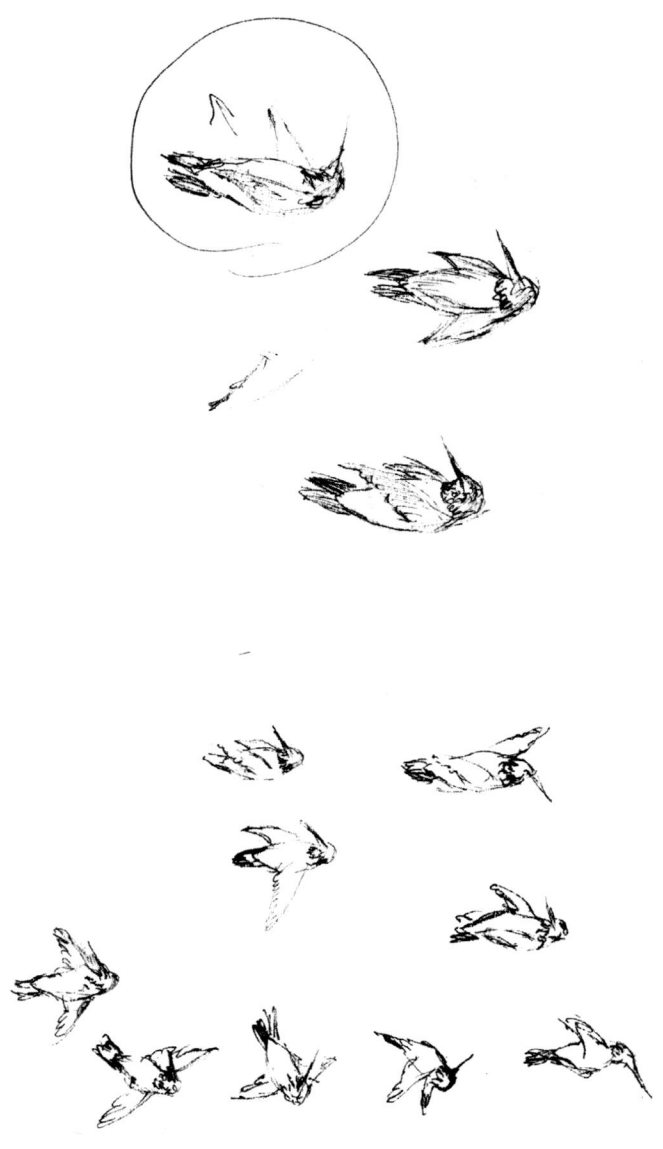

ghostly, angelic mating flight, anchored in reality through the quality of the artist's beautifully drawn line rendered with such directness on canvas. Here and elsewhere the birds appear as a metaphor for consciousness.

The artist is making a series of watercolors (p. 56-57) blooming with warm rose and white in which hummingbirds engage with birch trees. In one haunting piece, hummingbirds forever flicker, impossibly unrestrained but held, through a forest of birch trees. Elsewhere in this series a splendid green ground embraces a delicate female torso and a swan's head, bleeding [see Quiet Night (wind) III, p. 59].

In a profound way the intercourse between fish and feeder hummingbird (or potentially between the swan and viewer) represents in parallel that mystical interchange that one sees represented in Northwest Coast Indian art. For example, in carved ritual works of art, such as Tlingit or Haida rattles, one finds a reclining human shaman in mystic communion with a spirit helper frog, whose long tongue is in the shaman's mouth. On a large, carved, cedar wood screen by the late Haida artist Bill Reid, many totemic animals are in rapt communion through their interconnected tongues. Martínez Celaya's imagery arouses these and other extended meanings. [c.f. *Stones, Bones and Skin: Ritual and Shamanic Art*, 1976, and *Bill Reid*, Doris Shadbolt, 1986.]

Among his richly textured recent works, one of my favorites is *The Tiger of Corners*. On a square canvas, emerging from a ground of thickly painted, atmospheric mauve-colored oil, the head and beak of a hair-covered hummingbird with prominently painted eye appears as an erotically charged image. This piece and another freighted

A fish, a very earthly thing, is very much bound in reality. The fish gasping for air or looking for food takes on an aspect of need, an earthly need. It seems like the hummingbird is feeding the fish. There is something about the urgent way the hummingbird is trying to feed the fish...the image of the fish is more complicated because it comes out of a poem about my grandfather's glass top coffee table where a ceramic fish sat, the table is in the middle of my grandfather's living room which was always kept in the dark.

•••

...so that image of that fish jumping from the water was always jumping out of that darkened living room. In some ways the fish brings forward that other reality or even factual information about childhood. The fish anchors, then pulls the whole ship of childhood, not maybe as it is remembered... nor as it was felt, but very much as it was. There's something about that darkened living room and the fish jumping out of it looking so different than the rest.

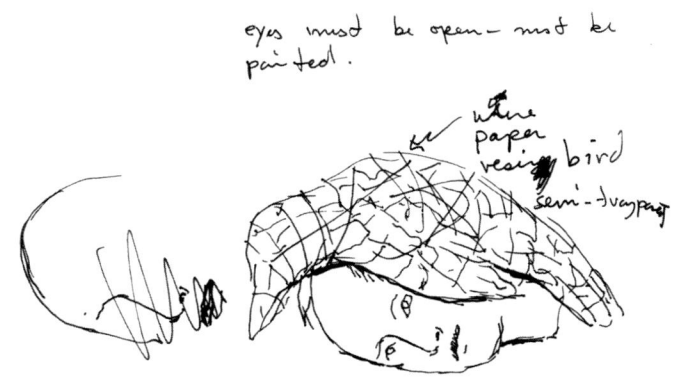

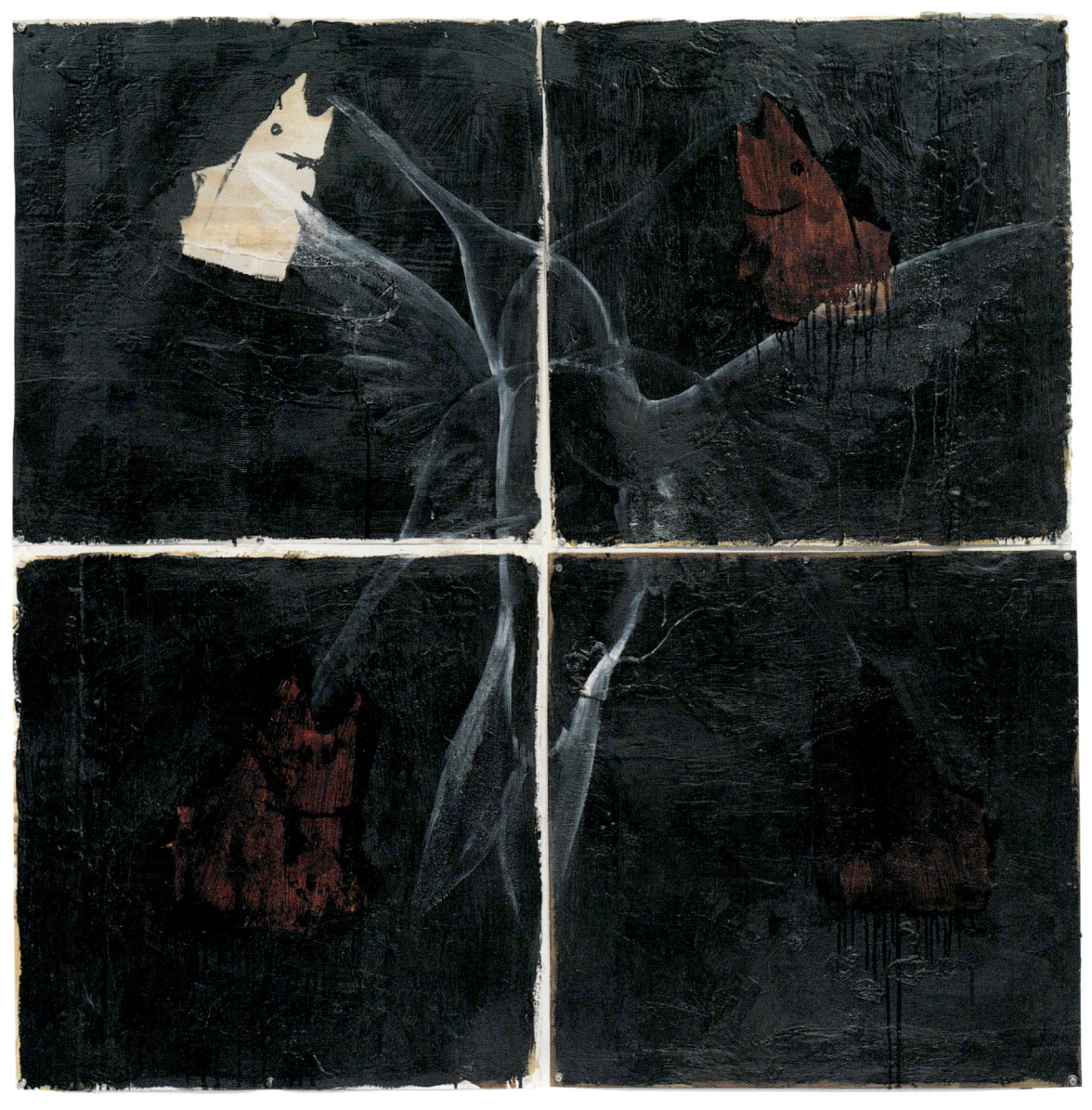

Feeder and Voice 1999

with perhaps darker meaning, *Broken Solitude*, recall some of the profound works of Ryder and Redon. The corners of the title recall a passage from one of Martínez Celaya's poems,

> NO SPACE is more empty
> than the corner
> I never noticed.

These works, both the poem and the painting, speak again of the nature of memory and its compression by distillation. They suggest a passage in Gaston Bachelard's *Poetics of Space*, 1964, where a whole chapter is devoted to corners, when the author remarks on the corner as a symbol of solitude for the imagination.

A major painting, approximately 8' x 8', shows two hummingbirds, no longer sweet, picking at a bleeding face, whose mouth is shaped like a flower. The contrast between the nearly ethereal white birds and the apparent violence of their activity suggests to Martínez Celaya something about the very process of meaning, its layered complexity, its multiplicity. The aggressive action of flapping wings connects with the aggressive movement of time.

This reference to time wherein the swiftness of the hovering birds is conflated with the notion of their licking of a wounded face as they would lick nectar from a blossom recalls the actual experiential compression that the artist describes in his conversation with M.A. Greenstein about Hegel's influence on his own thought.[†]

Perhaps in the experiencing of pain and loss in two other new paintings, we feel something of what the Greeks called *Paedeia*, wherein pain and its obverse release can be

... the hummingbird itself is this sort of defiant little animal that when you hold it, it's as if there is nothing there. It is so insignificant in weight but its flight makes you very aware that it is very alive. Its definite presence of life, and its evanescent quality of weight, makes it a living metaphor for consciousness. So on one level the hummingbird is that. It can also become the manifestation of the spirit or a good way to suggest the spirit. I think I like the fact that hummingbirds collapse the distance between the nostalgic and sentimental and the transcendental, often because they have been used traditionally as quaint imagery. Everybody has them on their refrigerators; they're cute, these little images of hummingbirds. There is that kitschiness in hummingbirds that introduces a wedge into much more serious considerations. I think somehow that the marriage of sentimentality and detachment implies a heightened poignancy which is much closer to the way I experience life. I like the fact that the juxtaposition of banality and seriousness can coexist within an image of a hummingbird. It is a wonderful surprise to find a very serious painting with a four foot by five foot hummingbird...much more surprising than a Campbell's soup can.

[†]*See interview in <u>Berlin, The Fragility of Nearness</u>, 1998.*

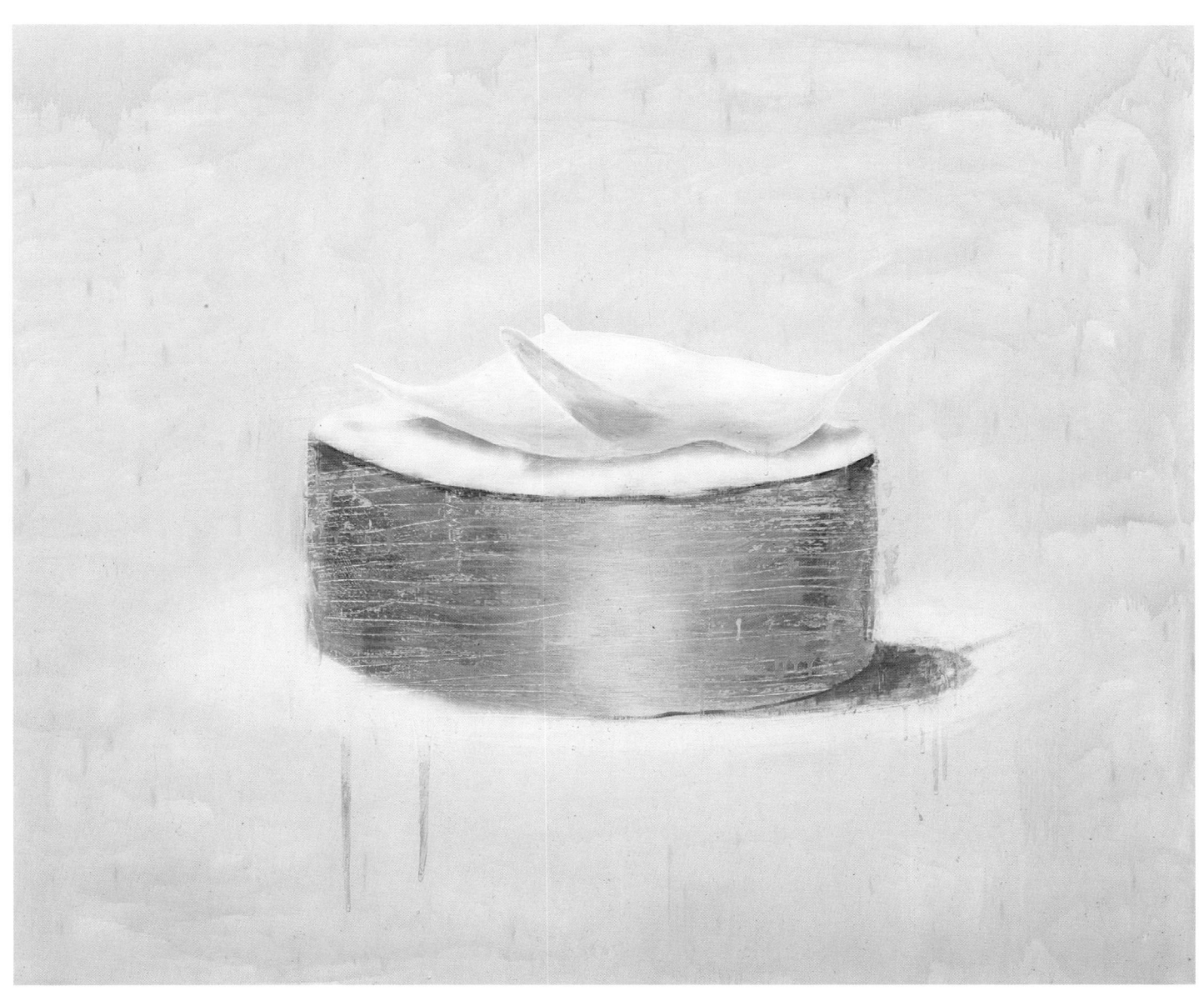

Acceptance of Longing 1997
Los Angeles County Museum of Art, Los Angeles

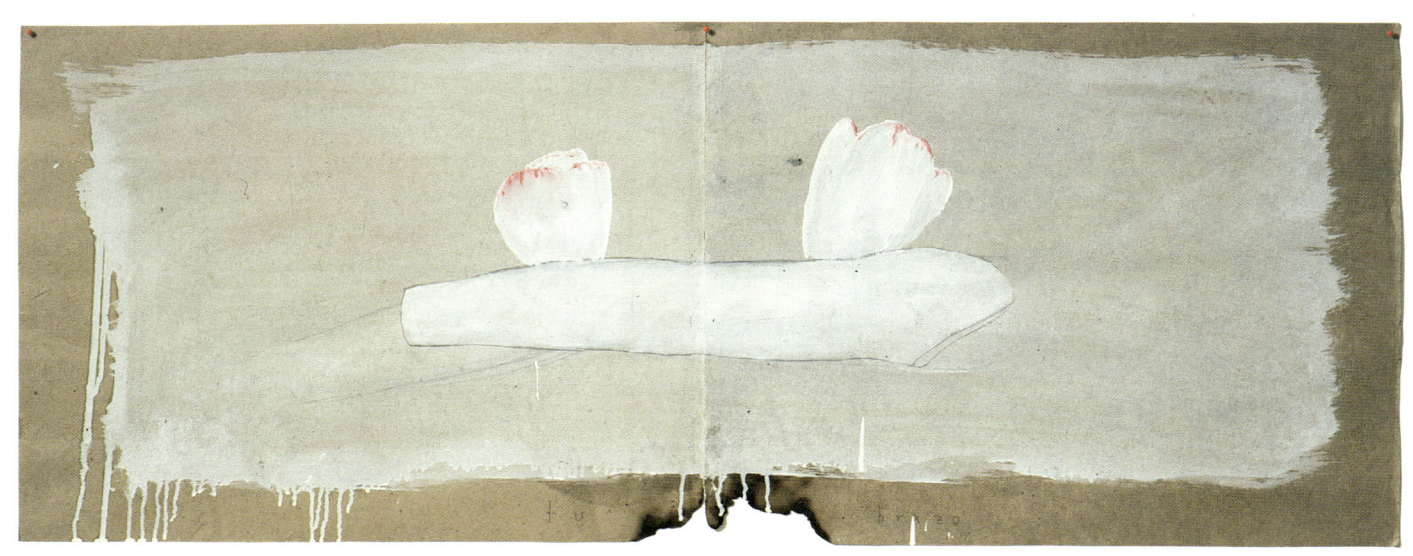

Tu Brazo (your arm) 1997

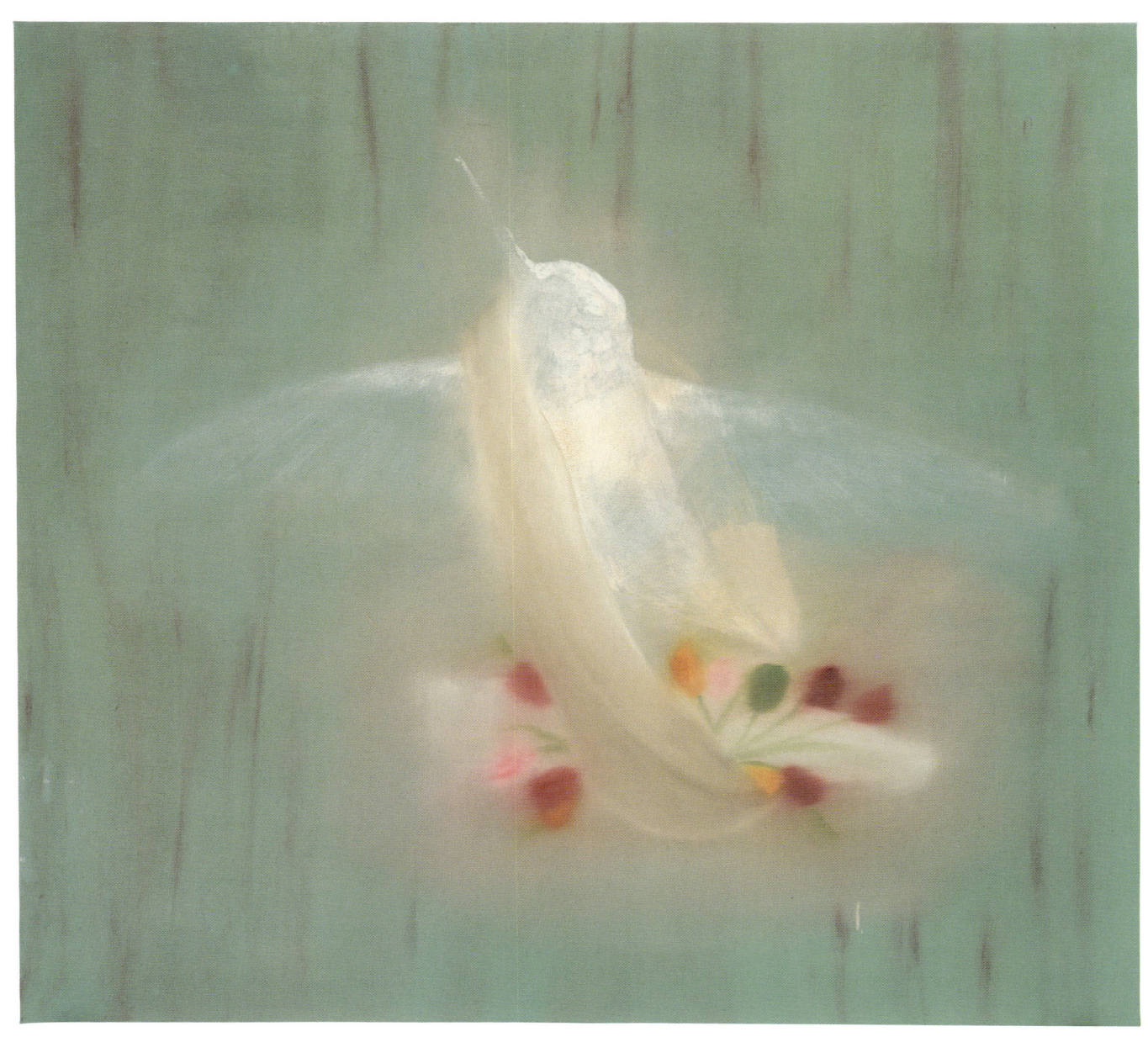

Vanity and Redemption 1997

experienced in an almost ennobling way, in the sense of tragedy, in the sense of enlargement. In the first, titled *Broken Solitude*, a hummingbird flops down, wings back, folded into what may be the embrace of large tears. Written on the reverse of the painting are the words, "the collapse brought on by tears of confidence."

The second painting of tragic import, among the most romantic and achingly beautiful of recent works, is *Black Hummingbird, White Birch* (p. 49). Here the bird impaled on a sharpened stake droops, surrounded by a mist of pink light and seen against a dark ground where the curve of a wrought iron fence may enclose a garden. The painting, the sheer gigantic scale of the bird in relation to the tree, the compacted image, recalls memories of violence, of war, of Goya's use of color and livid light, mingled with the tragic sense of a life, so vivid and so expressive of consciousness, lost. Yet the evanescent rosy colors of life remain as a mystery.

Mysterious and metaphysical, though hardly as dark, are the immense pair of paintings mentioned above, *Pena* (p. 55) and *The Empty Garden*: a hand in one reaching across white space to a head reclining in the other. Immensity is conveyed in these two images through sheer scale but also, and more fervently, through the wonderful luminous viscosity of tar painted over wax and oil. Around the wrist of the outstretched hand is a bracelet or cuff made of real flowers, ribbons, baby shoes, plastic lilies, tar and feathers, like a primal mass.

One returns once more to the artist's invocation of Melville, *Moby Dick* in particular, for here we see the artist dealing with the "idea of vastness versus smallness, the

...when you go to your parents' yard and you see the gardenias that your mother liked. In the moment that you smell them memory does a strange thing. In that moment maybe the trip to the yard is fractured in time. Two experiences exist at once. They are felt simultaneously. Multiple layers of history are compressed. How would you describe that experience? I am not interested in describing it. I am interested in going through that experience to reach the state where those two moments can coexist at once. [Conversation in *Berlin: The Fragility of Nearness,* 1998.]

Stonewall 1997 ▶

36

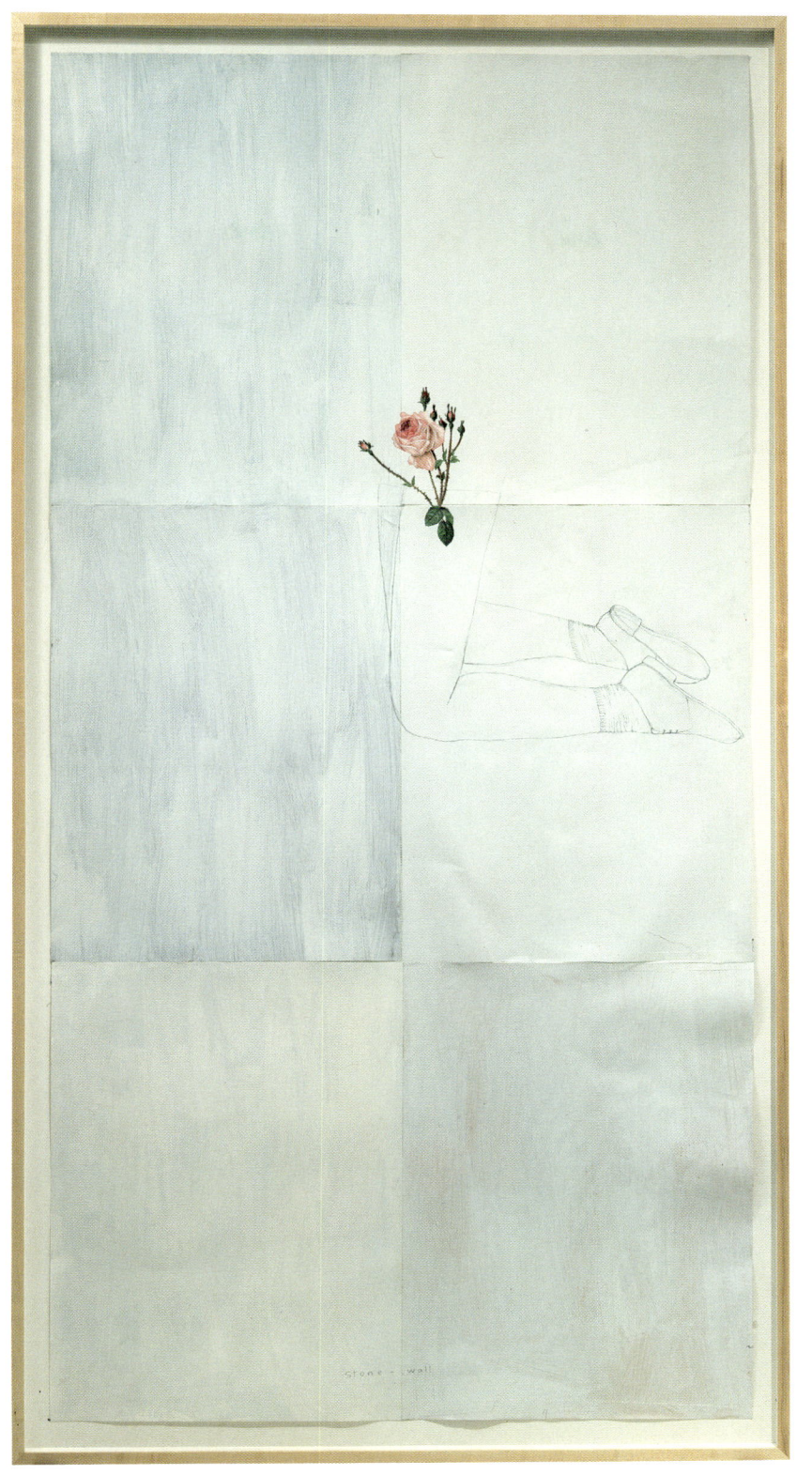

larger quest of life. He is interested in the brutality and beauty of *Moby Dick*. Can one combine in a single gesture brutality and grace?"

In Martínez Celaya's studio one finds other monumental works: a swan's head superimposed on a huge field of actual brown, amber, and plum colored rose petals; a giant crimson rose petal in another painting reposing on a white bed, its fragrance or blood leaves traces on a pillow; a black swan, its beak made of golden rose petals mounted over a maze that threatens to engulf it. Such opulent paintings as these line the walls of his studio, and on the floor, immense heads recline, commenting urgently, even in their unfinished state, on the imagery in the work.

Three pieces are particularly compelling in light of the themes of memory, loss, and reconciliation that so clearly imbue the meaning and the making of all of these works. In the first, *Master Song* (p. 72), a great swan, its head and neck centered, iconic, Byzantine in poise, extends from its visionary eye a challenge to clarity, to consciousness. Emerging from a scumbled ground of sandy, no-color color, dry and arid, this gloriously drawn, totemic swan wears around its neck five white pearls, each of which act as a full stop to the written words:

Senseless   Bruiseless   Needless   Secretless   Fateless

The swan's highly representational eye, worthy of a Vermeer, holds the reflection of a window. In the second work, *Open Sky, the Feeder* (p. 61), pink tulips and a white blossom are the ambient, painterly matrix for the gentlest of reclining or dreaming heads upon which play the iridescent figures of a leaping, open-mouthed fish and the similarly hued green-gold flicker of the hummingbird that feeds

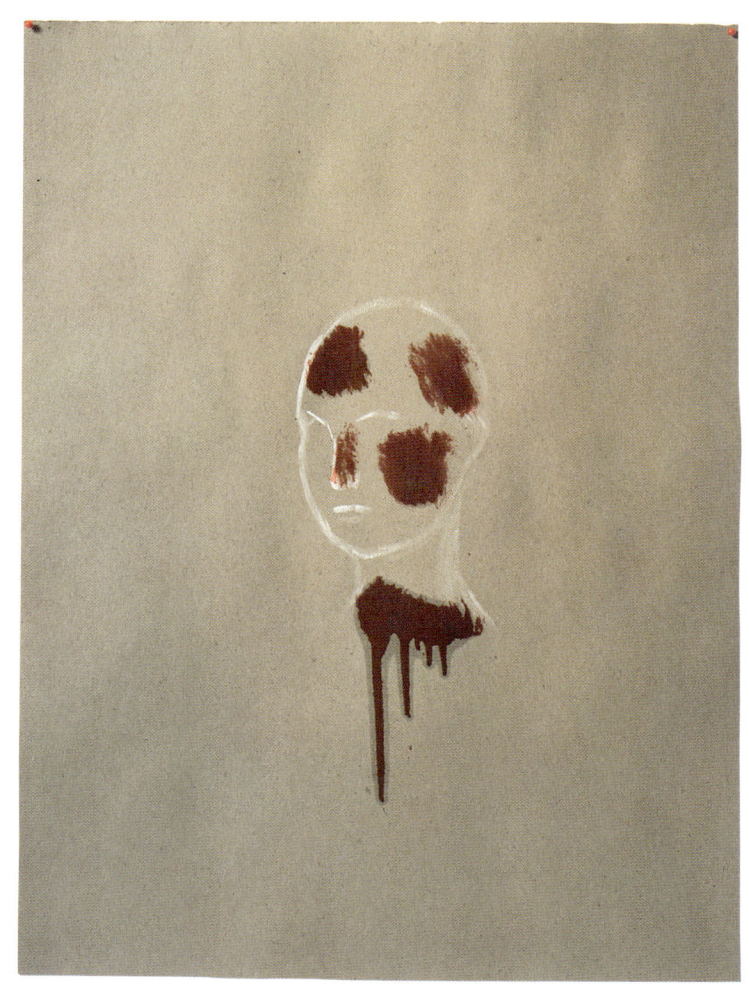

A boy in his room 1997   The Secrets 1997

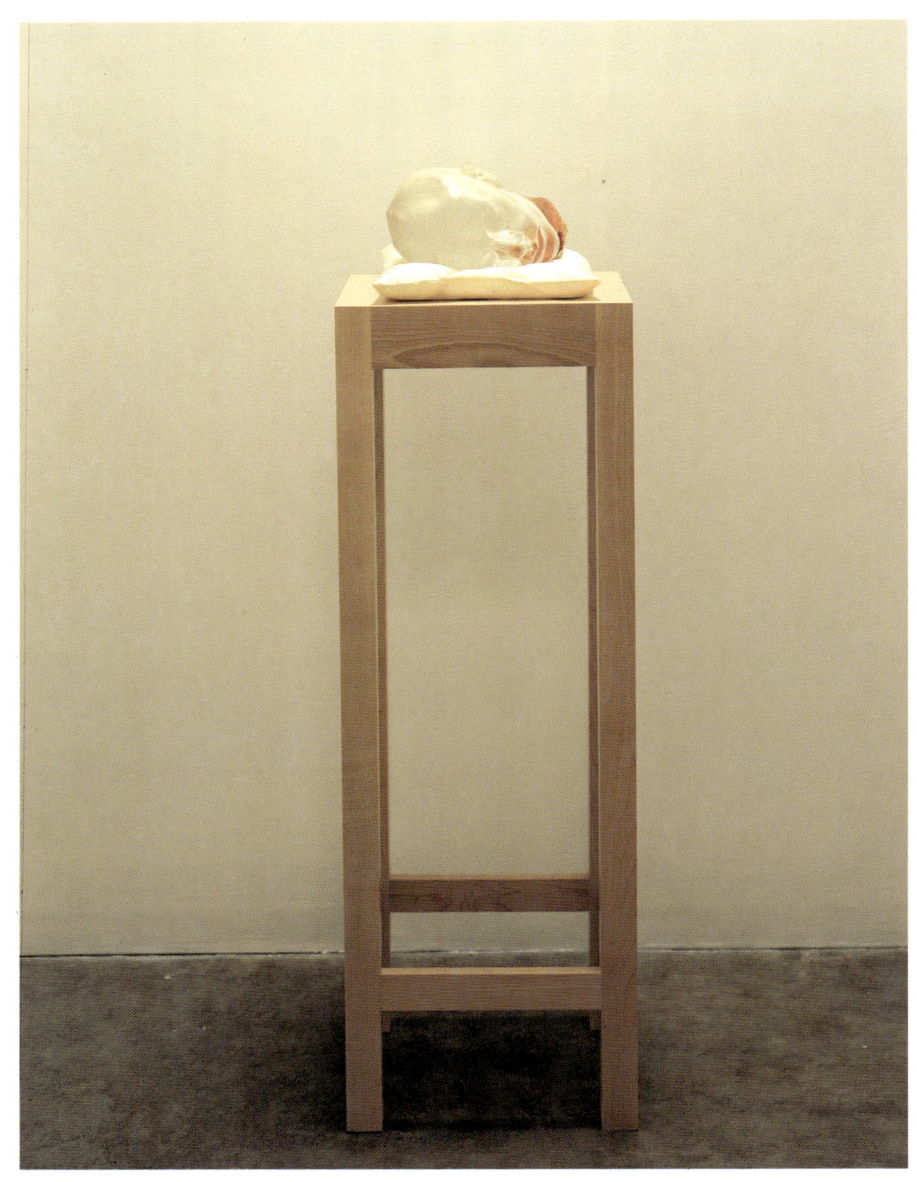

St. Catherine (Absolution) 1997

him. Their bodies, or the motion they create, obscure the dreamer's eyes, yet their eyes regard each other in mystic communion. And finally, in *Unbroken Poetry* (p. 63), Martínez Celaya's great, serious, archaic, dark-brown hummingbird flies rampant in a field of rosy light leaving earth stains on the translucent milky white tissue of his ether/ground. This painting, with the smudges of its making, with the emanations of clear rosy light from the bird's body and wings, with its far-seeing mystic eye, seems to figure forth and foretell its spirit of awareness, of presence, of consciousness. It shares that spirit of American art found in the best work of Morris Graves, of Ralph Waldo Emerson or Herman Melville at its ecstatic extreme.

The unbroken poetry of the process itself of distilling memory and the slow down-dropping of meaning that one begins to extract from the ongoing, interrelated works by Enrique Martínez Celaya, is life giving. His work is about meaning. He is an artist concerned with value in art and literature. He speaks of the compression of two opposing elements, loss and transcendence of loss, memory and its fixedness.

> It's like if you take two kinds of rice and mix them together and shake them. You can identify that there are two different kinds of rice in the bowl, but they are so intermixed, they are so inseparable, that you cannot just simply pour one out. Reality is like this, it is an interwoven fabric that might best be desribed by its component threads. But once the threads have been woven into the fabric of life, the funny part about it is that you can't remove a single thread or the material will unravel. Unless you go for the boldness of the whole, you don't have any part of it.

Enrique Martínez Celaya is going for the boldness.

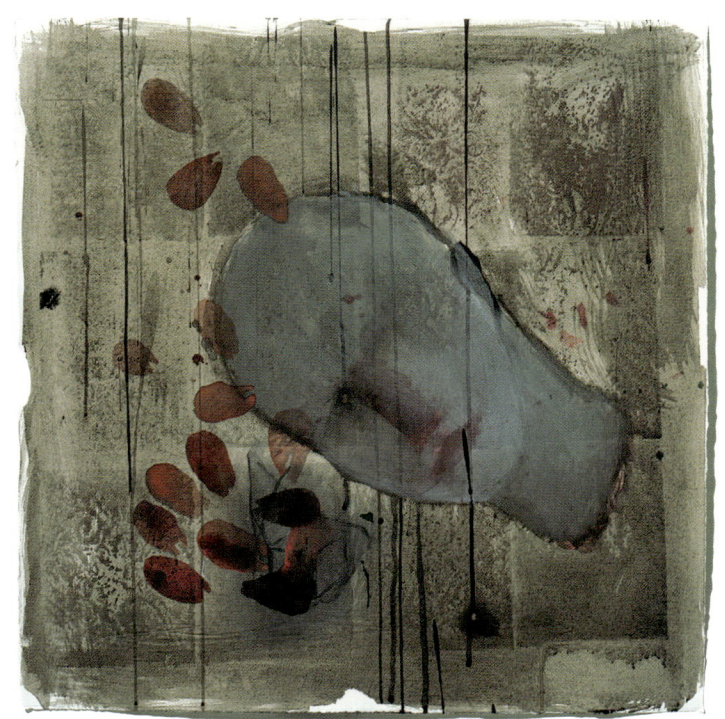

The most fragile 1998

41

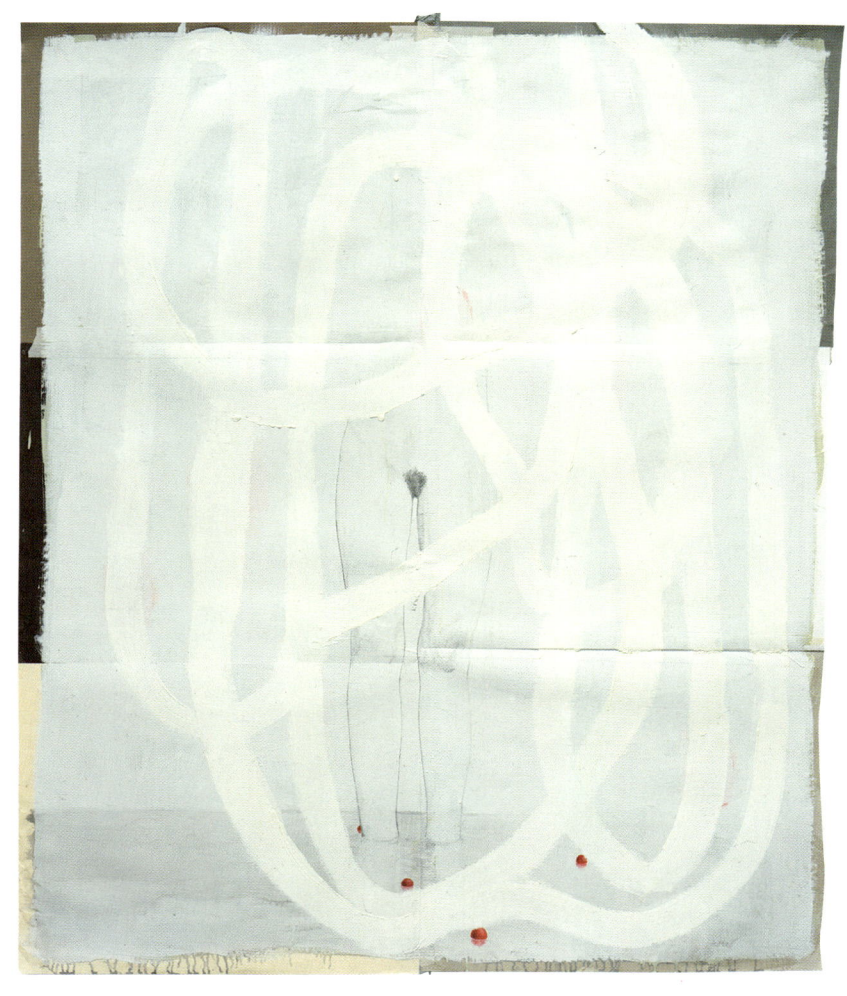

First War 1998

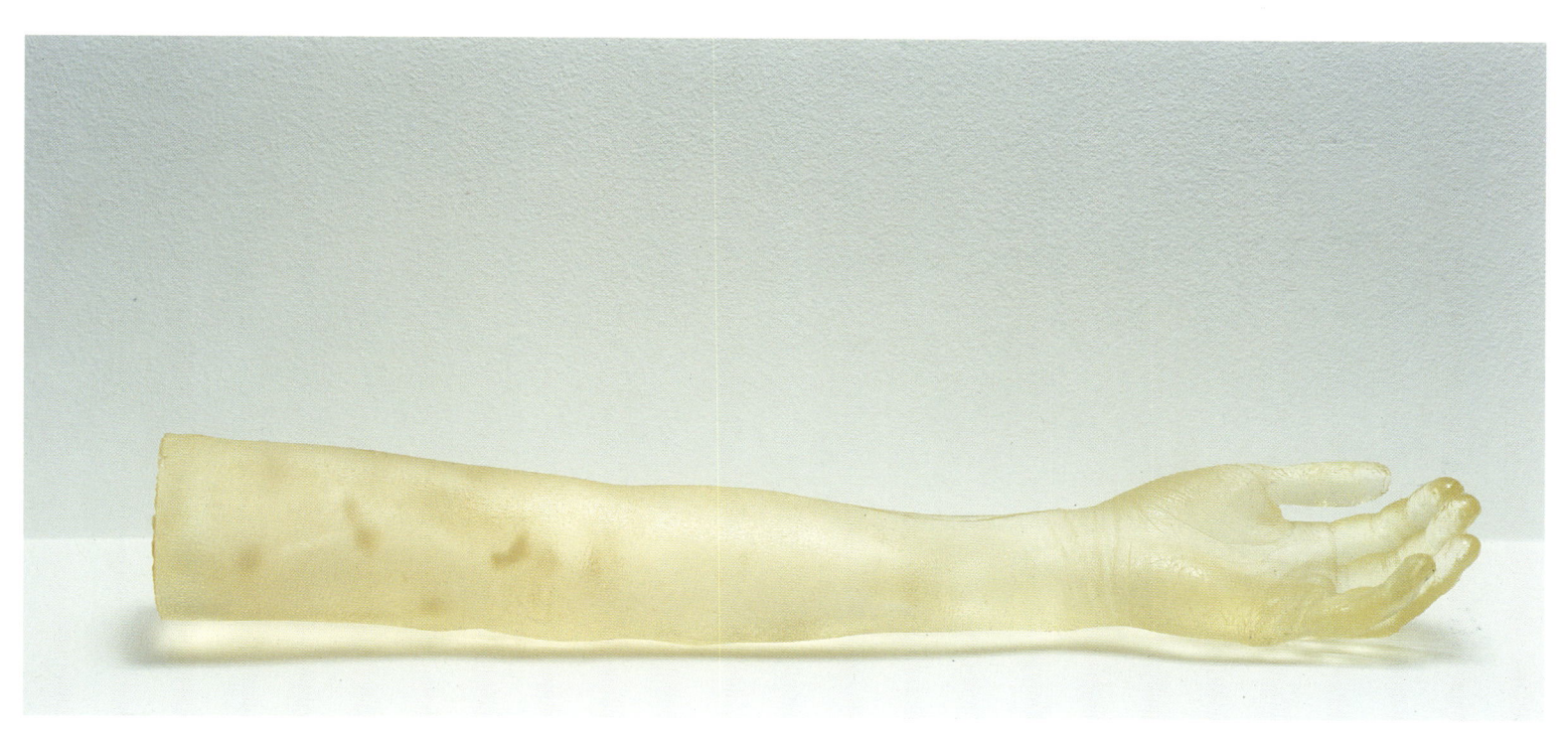

Marker 1997

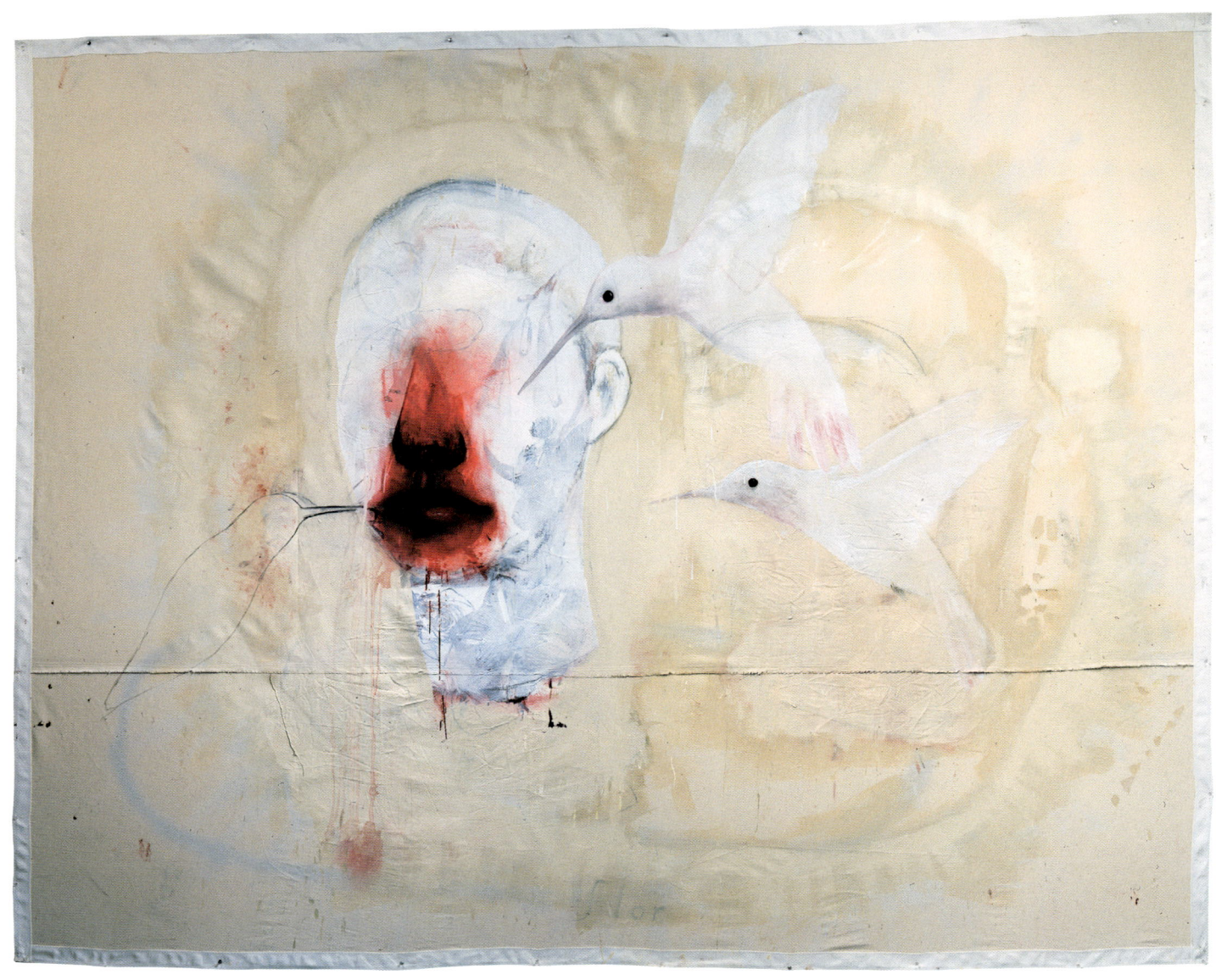

Quiet Night (recollection) I 1999

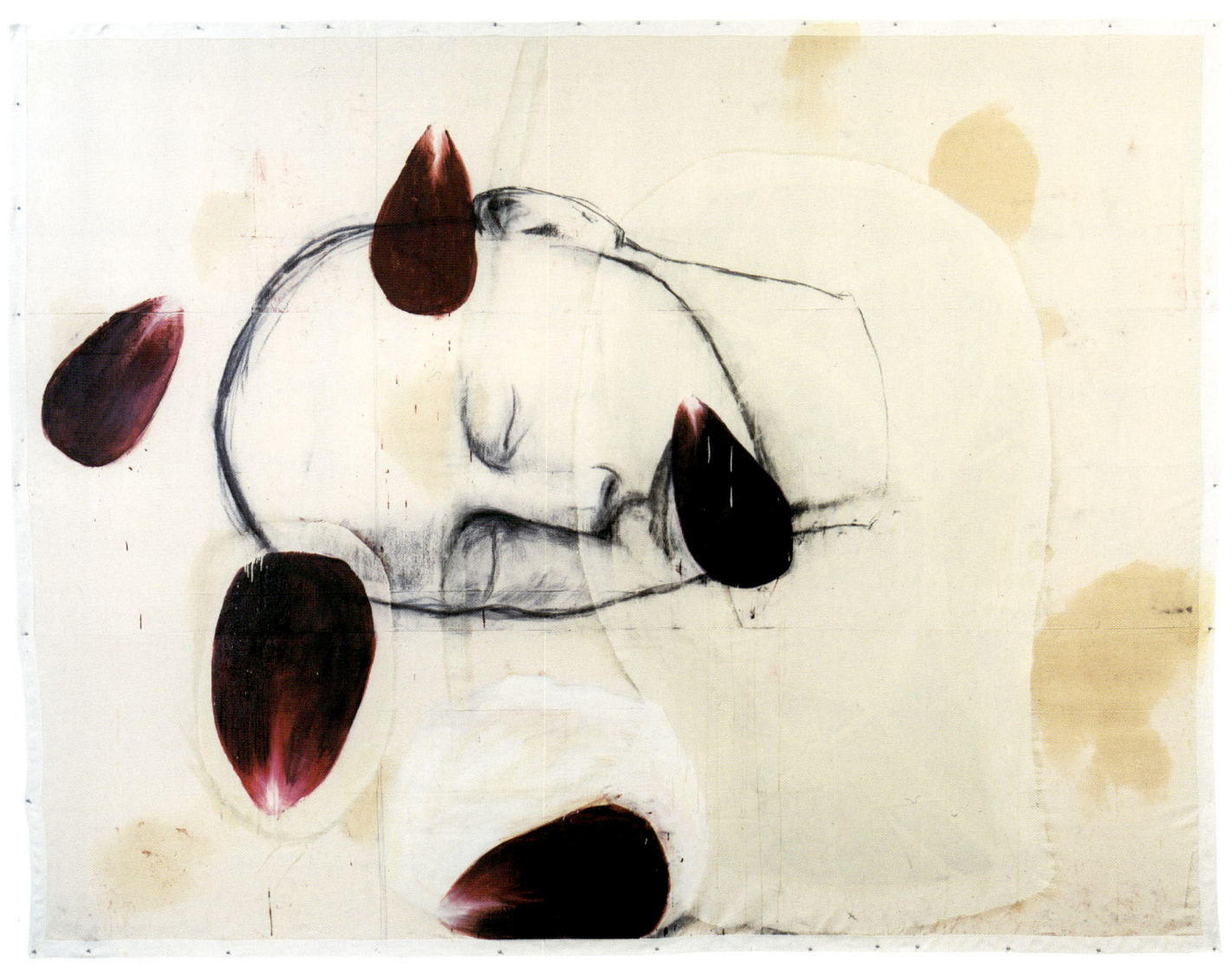

Quiet Night (recollection) II 1999

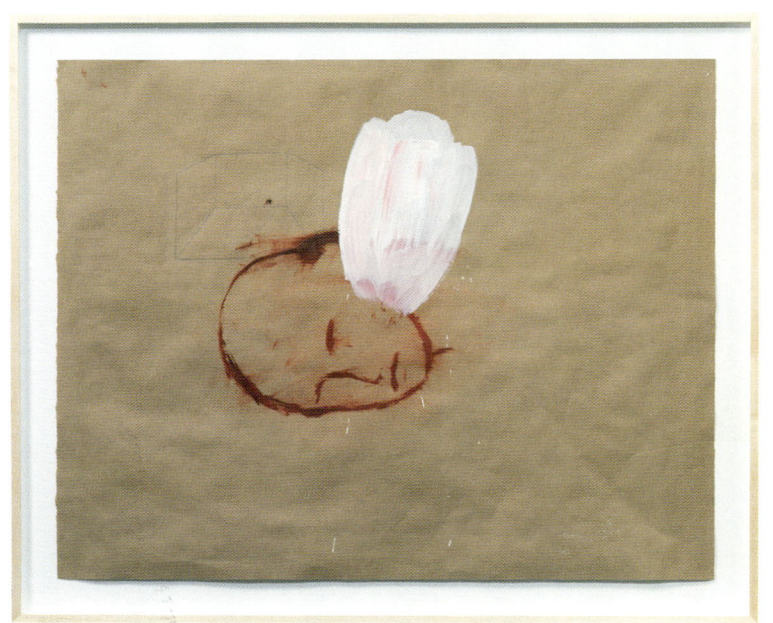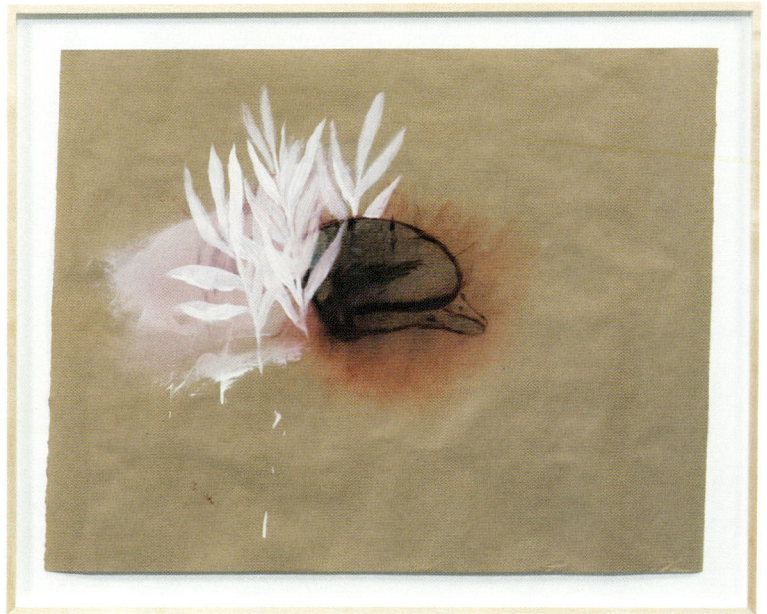

A Neck in Ashes 1997

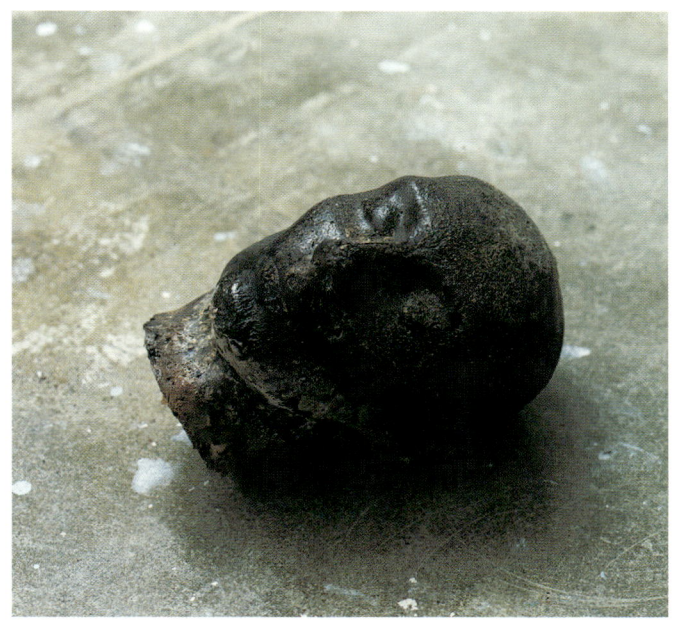

Half Again, Flower 1998

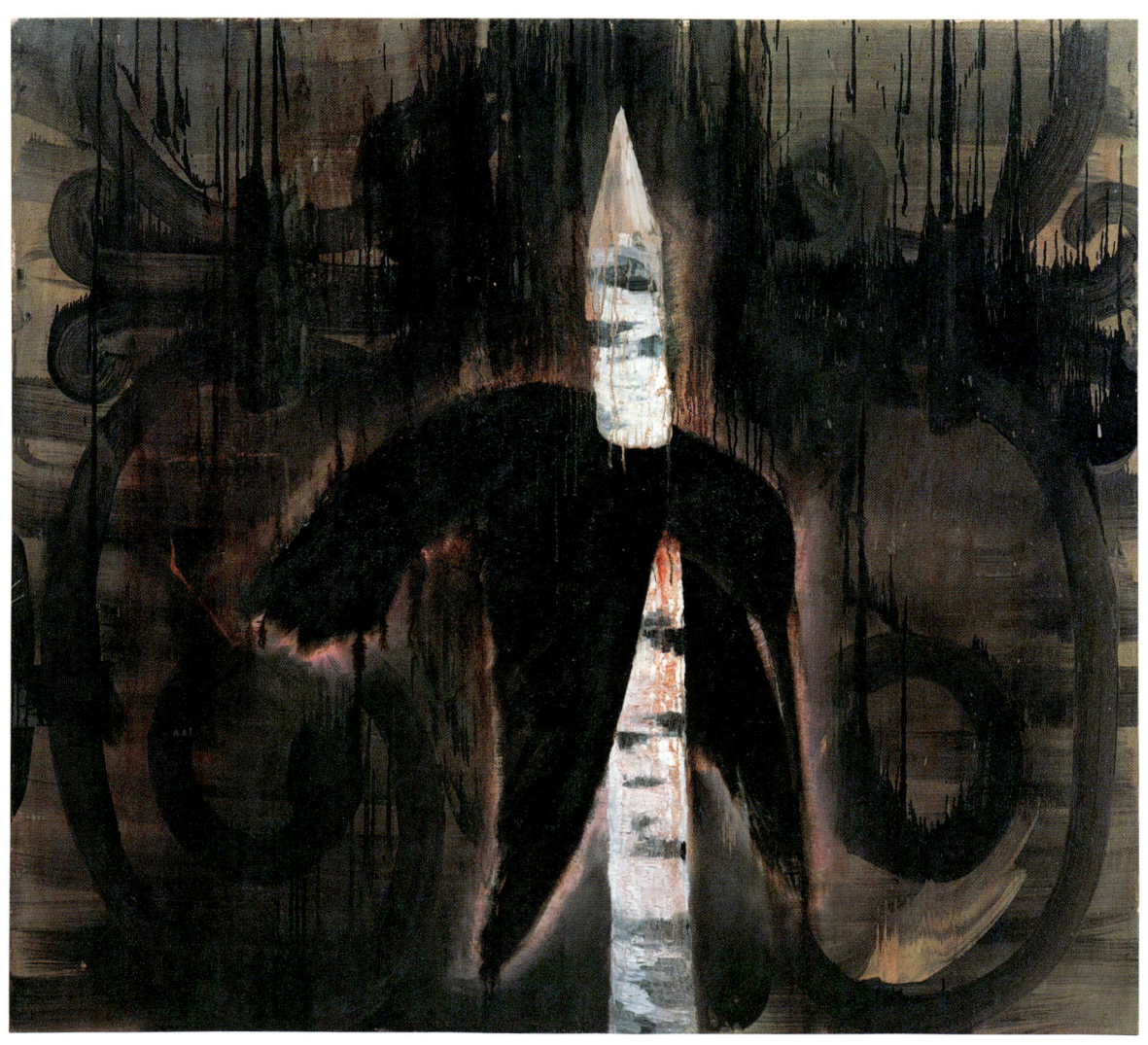

Black Hummingbird, White Birch 1999

The Undeniable and Unfortunate Truths 1998 ▶
Installation at Griffin Contemporary, Venice

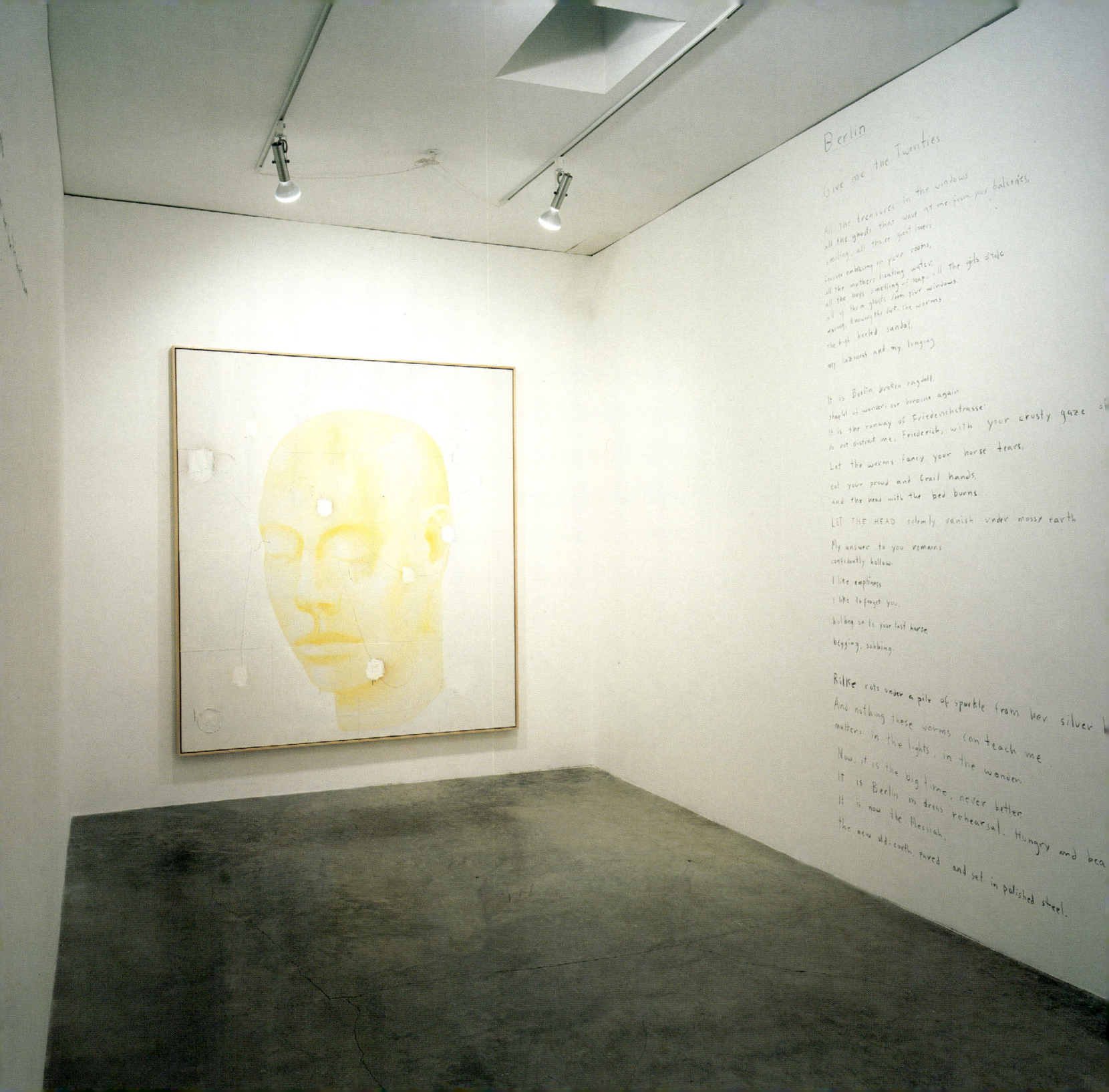

A Dry Bed 1998

A portfolio of ten ink drawings. A number and a line of text is written in graphite at the bottom of each drawing.

From left to right per row.

1. The imperfect future

2. must find me extinguished

3. trying to make sense

4. of faults and lack of meaning

5. of regrets

6. and people inevitably left behind

7. and irretrievable moments with them

8. this is then the past,

9. and I, a counter.

10. (No text)

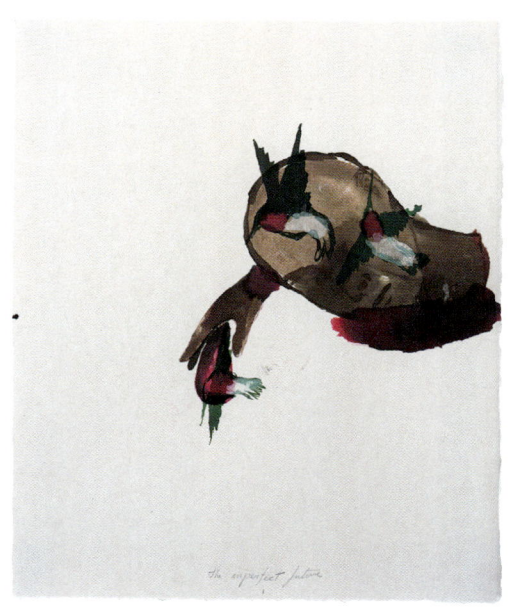
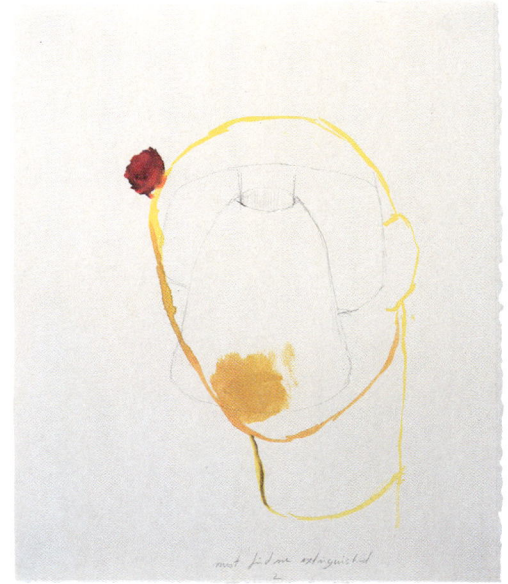
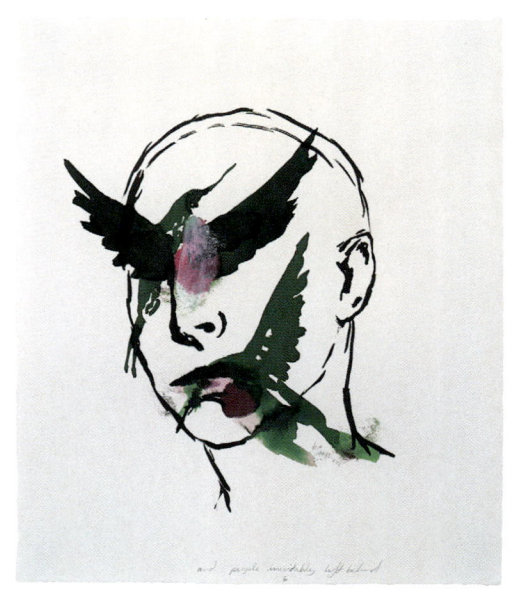
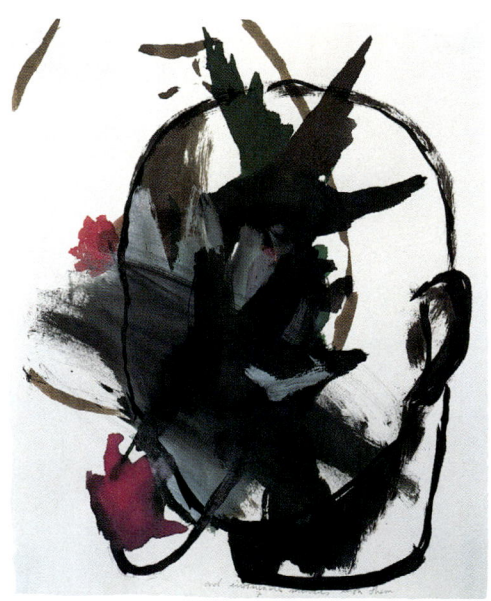

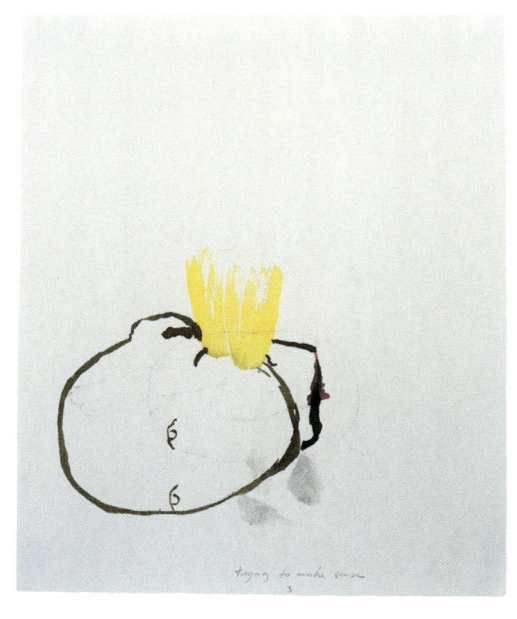

trying to make sense
3

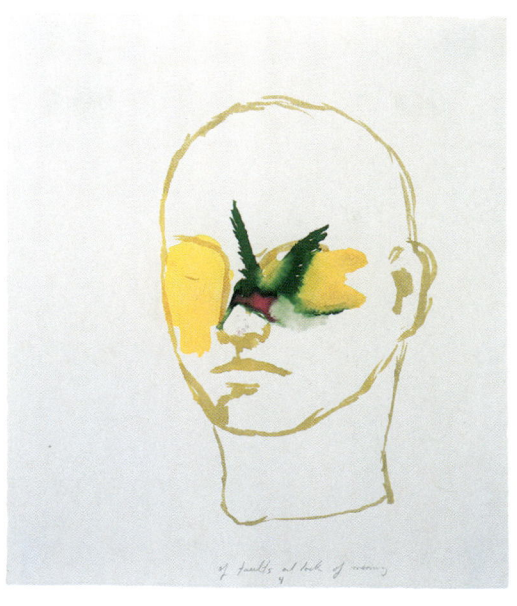

of faults at lack of meaning
4

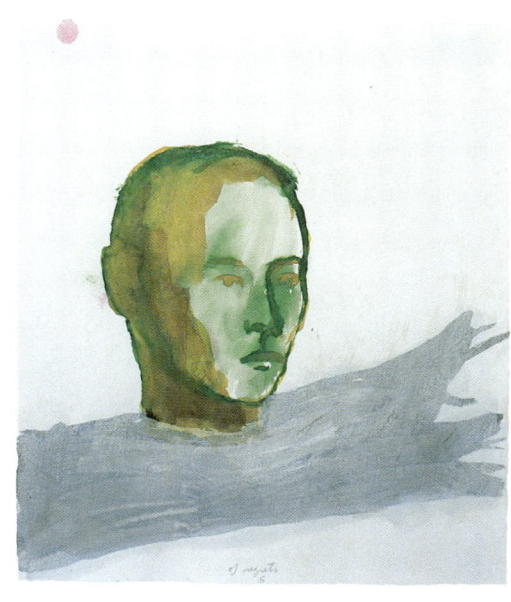

of regrets
5

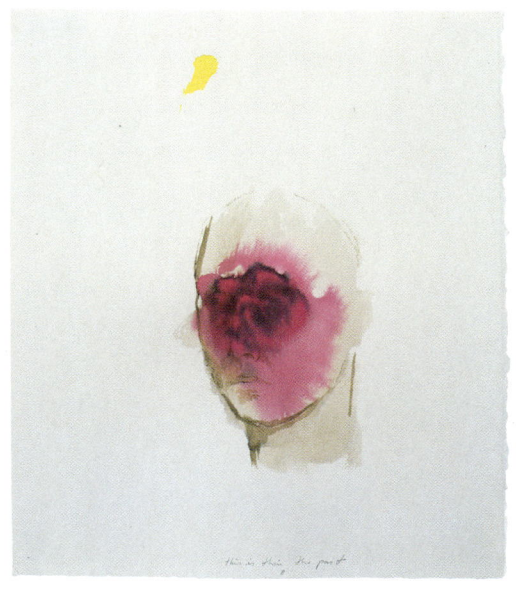

this is this the past

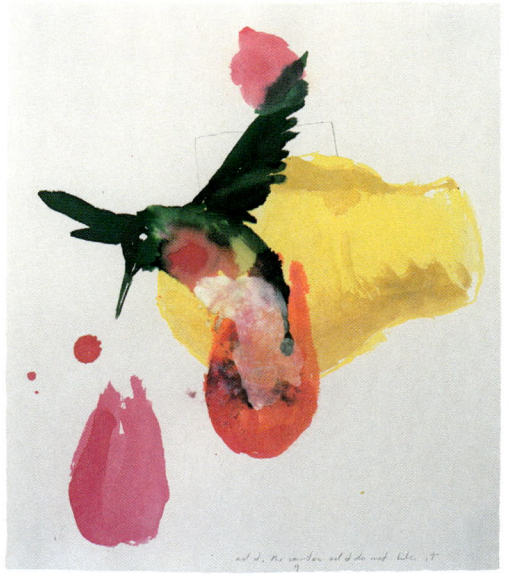

and I, the author and I do not like it
9

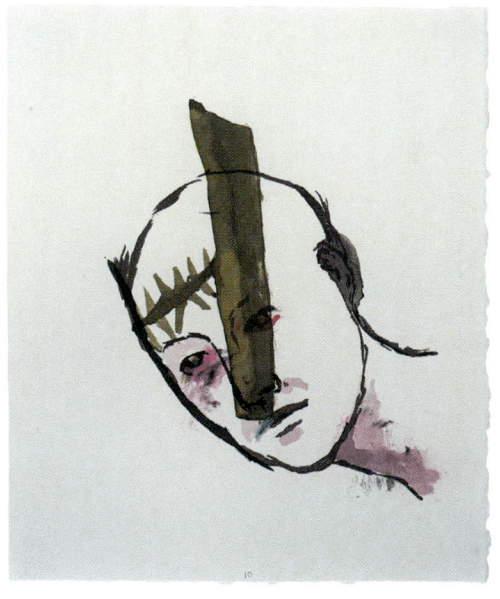

10

Pena 1999 ▶

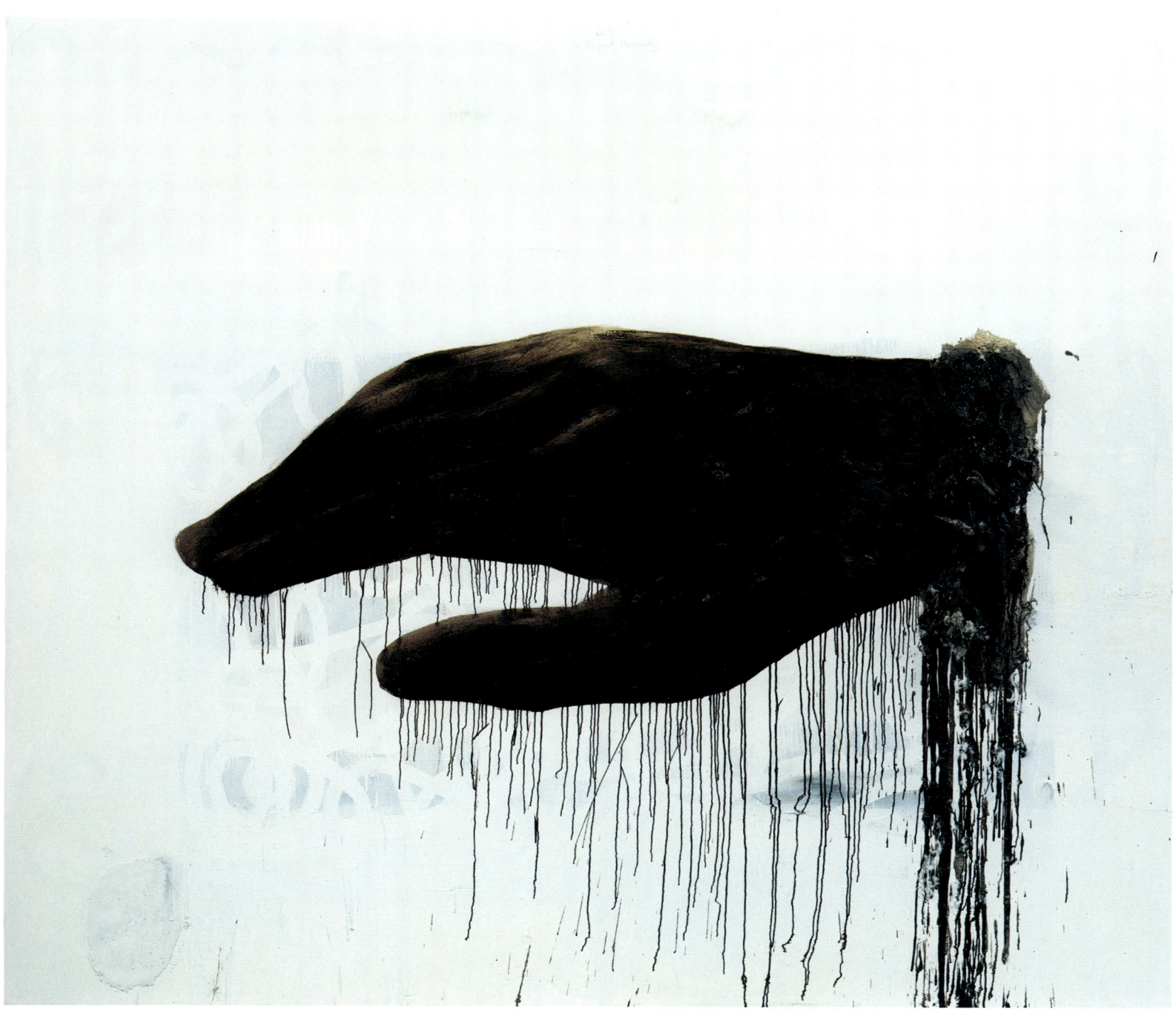

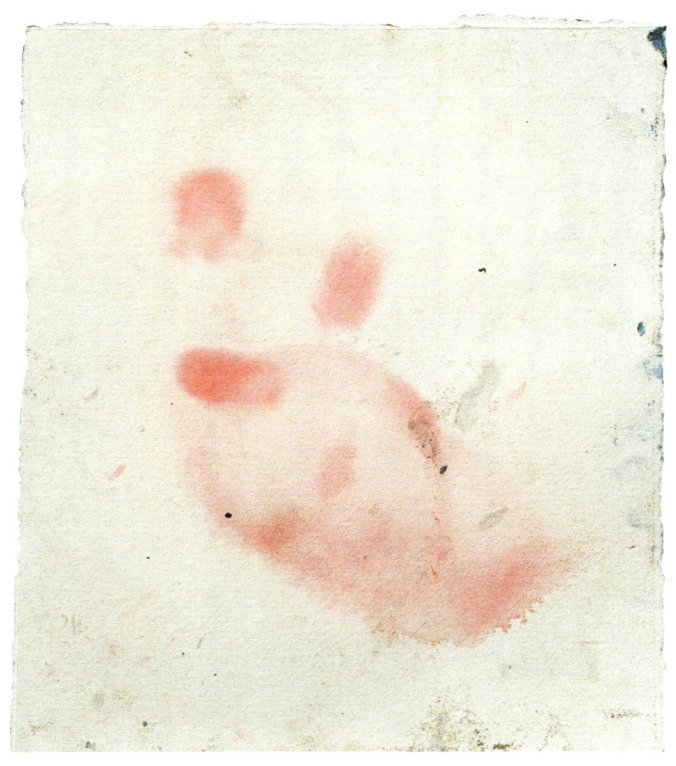

Skin for the Morning I (this page), II, III, IV, V (facing page) 1999

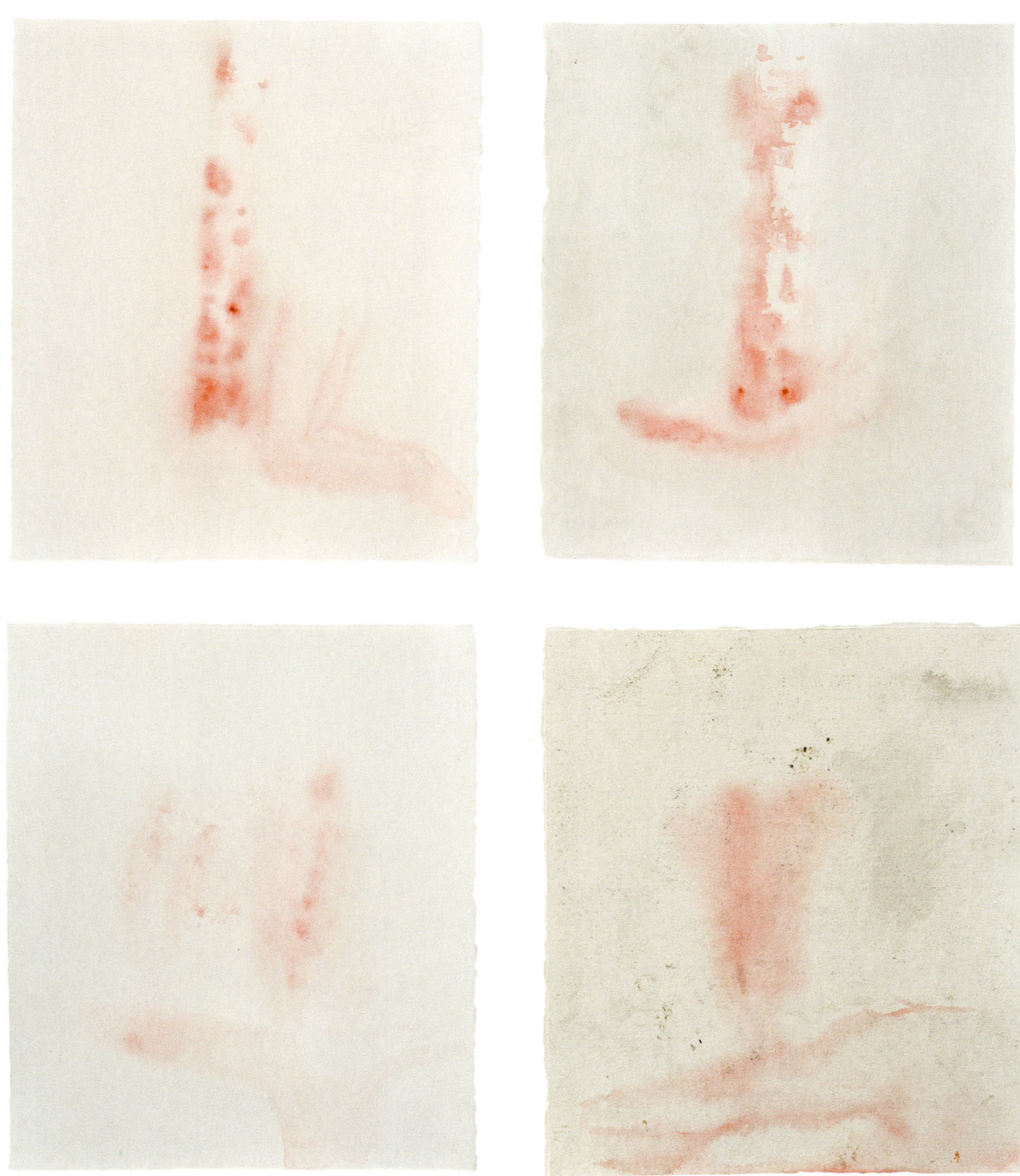

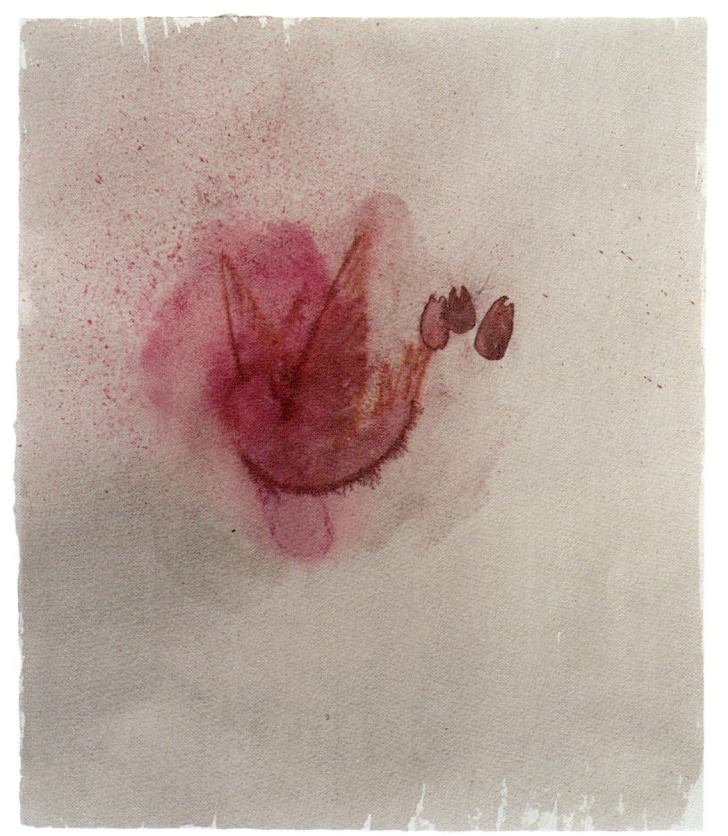

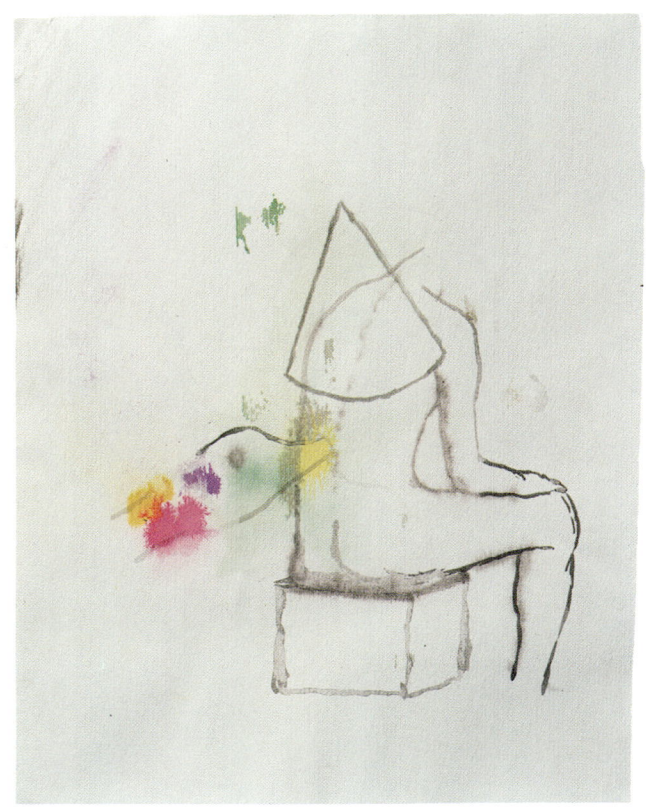

Quiet Night (wind) II 1999　　　　　　　　　Quiet Night (wind) V 1999

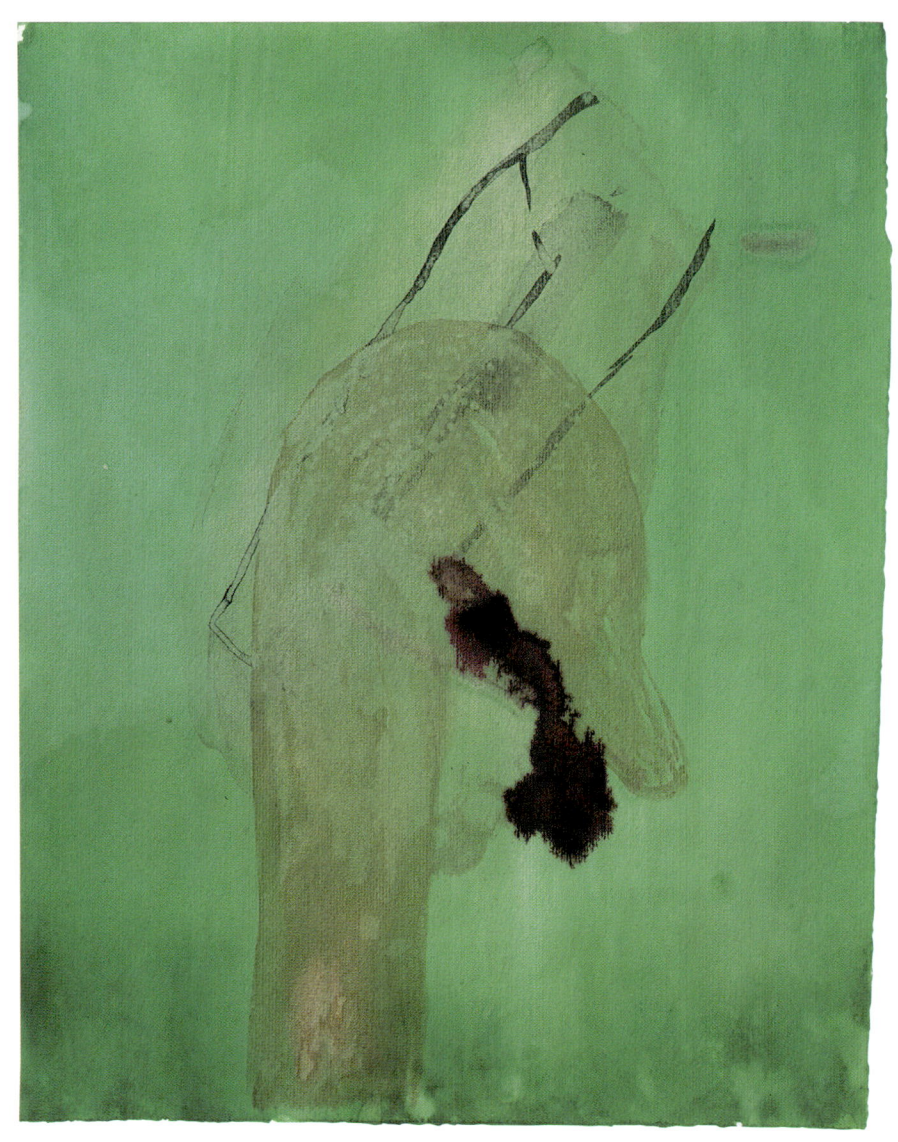

Quiet Night (wind) III 1999

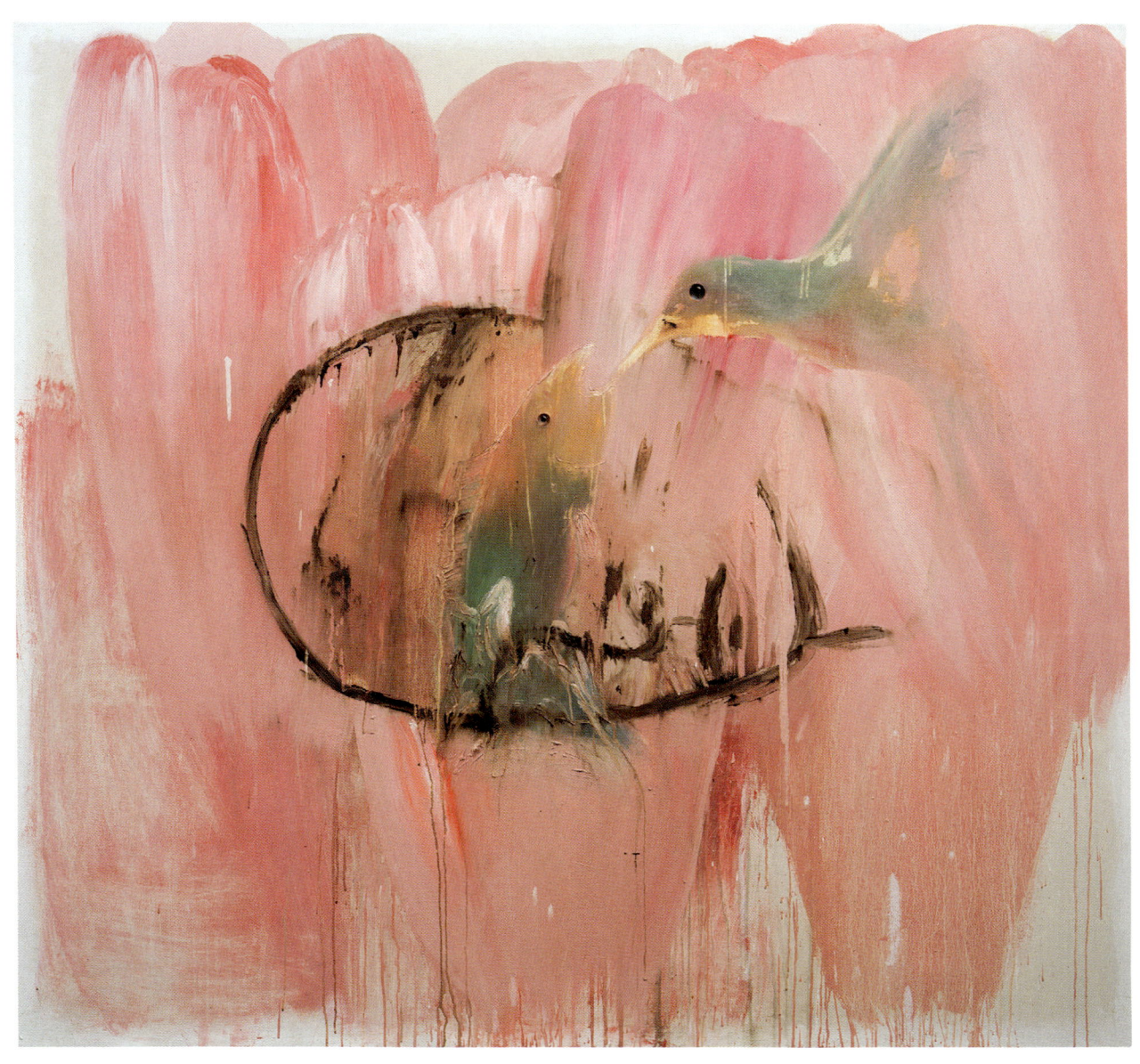

Open Sky, the Feeder 1999

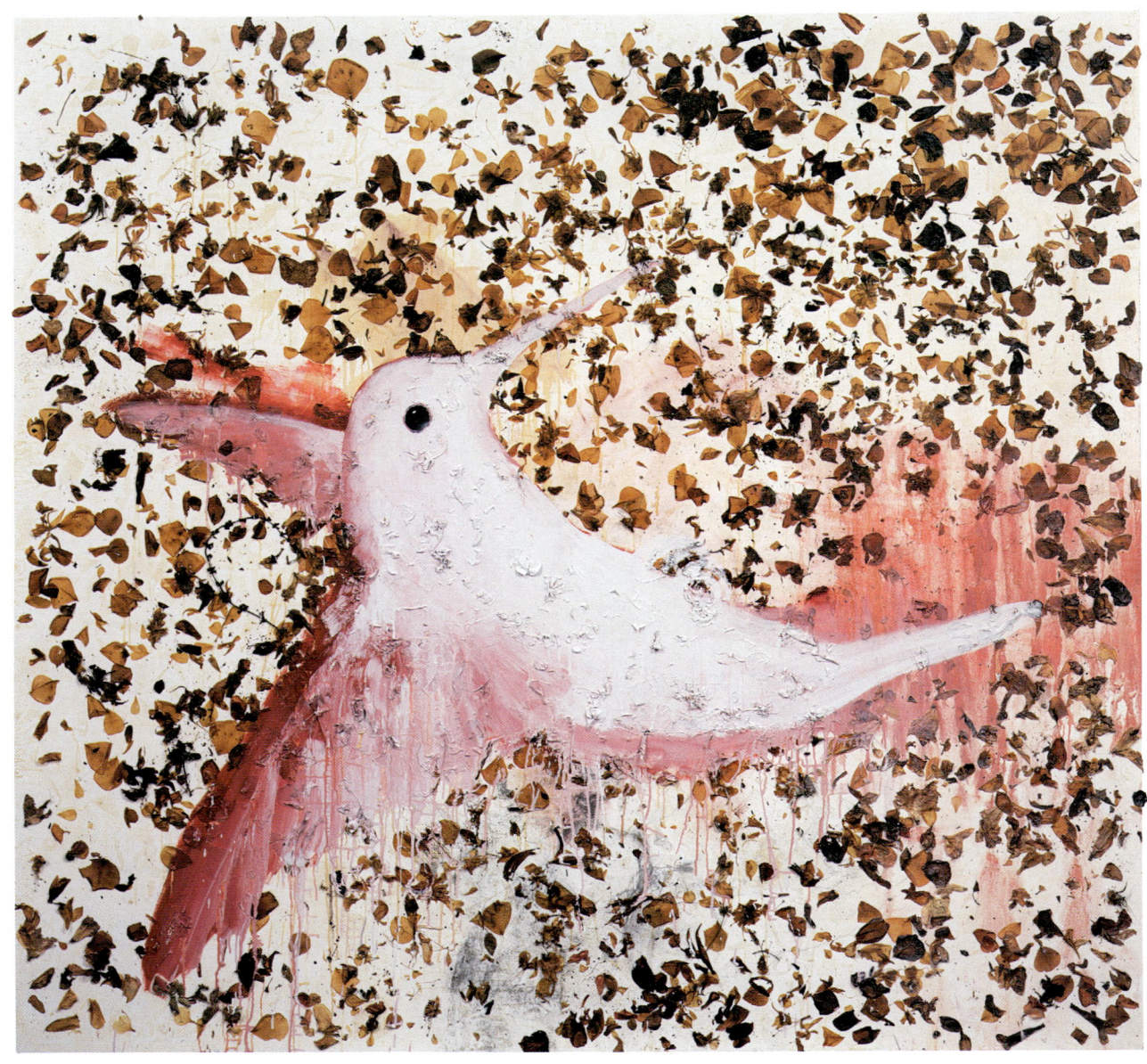

The Fall, Absolution 1999

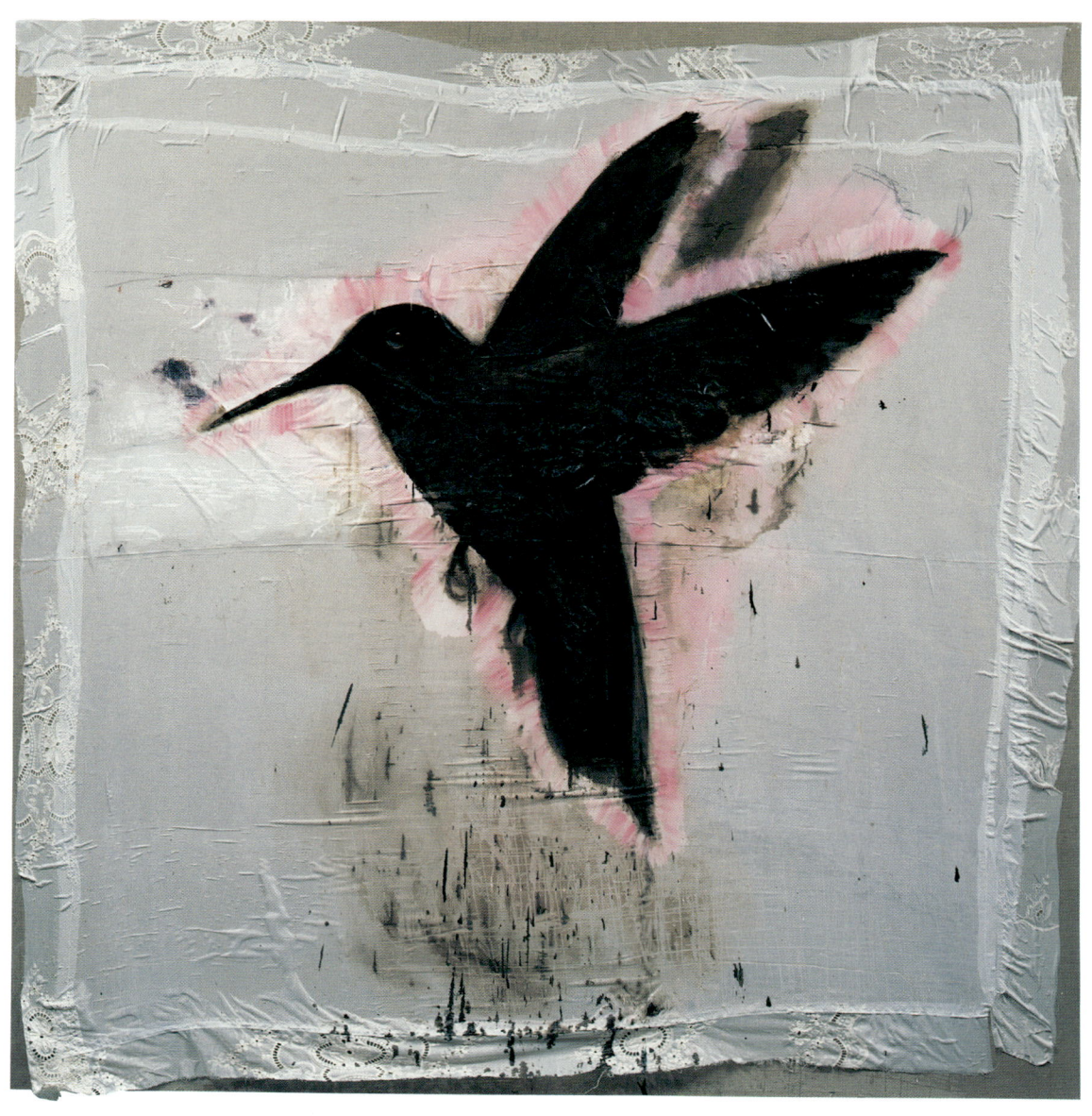

Unbroken Poetry 1999

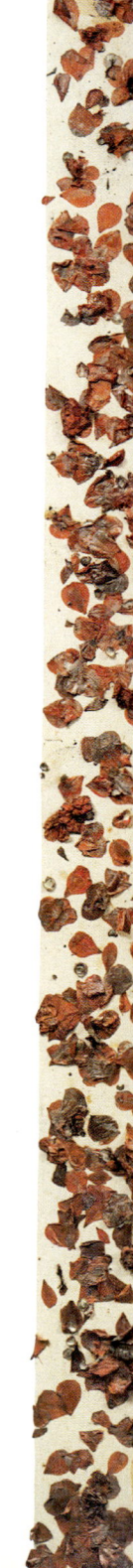

The Field 1999 ▶

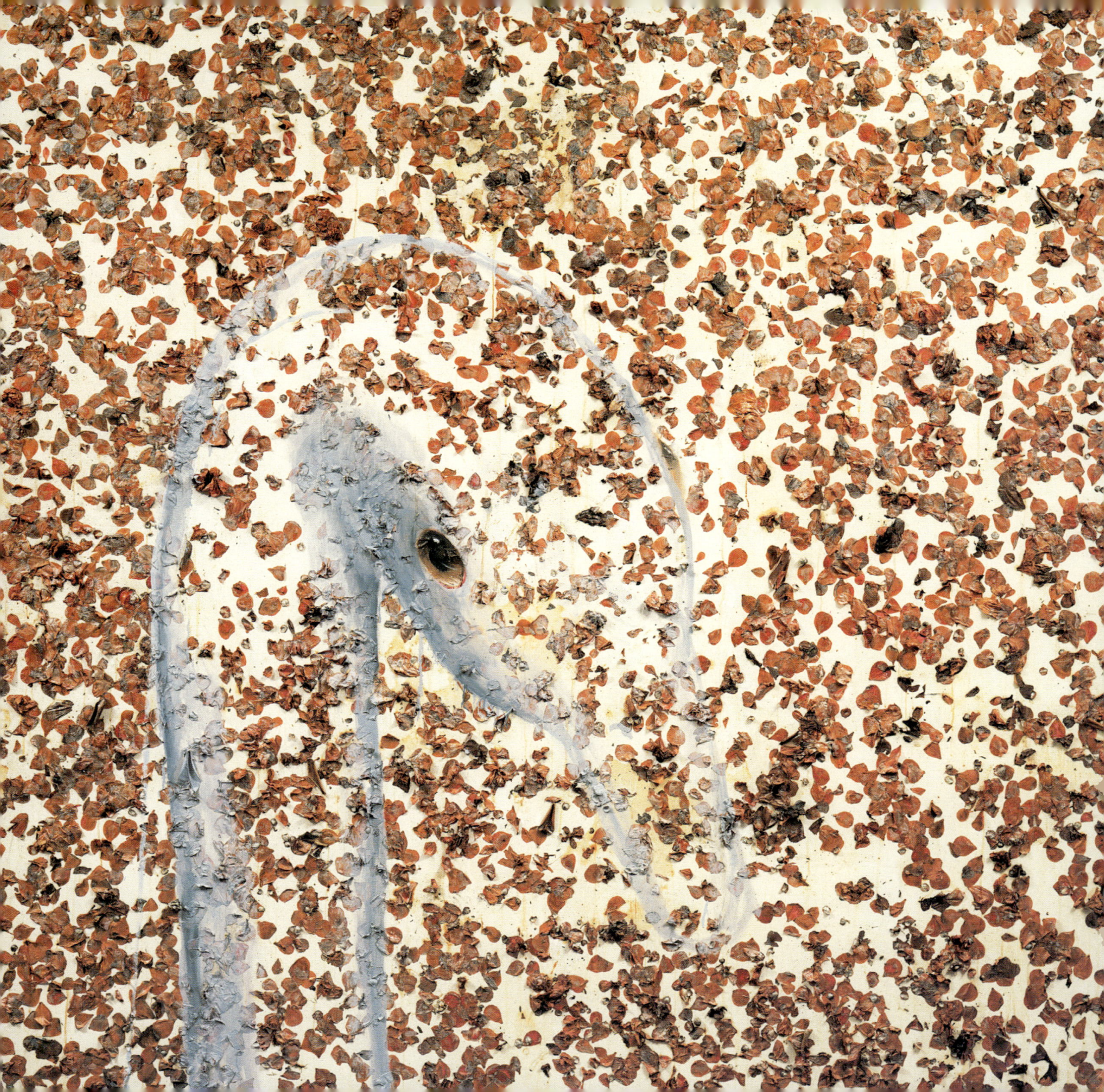

2 – Schroedinger equation.

(1) $\quad v = v(\omega, P) = \dfrac{\hbar\omega}{\sqrt{2m}}\dfrac{1}{\sqrt{\hbar\omega - U}}$

Monochromatic wave equation

$$\nabla^2\psi - \frac{1}{v^2}\frac{\partial^2\psi}{\partial t^2} = 0$$

(comments: need to assume fixed ω)

(2) $\quad \psi = u\, e^{-i\omega t} = u\, e^{-\frac{i}{\hbar}Wt}$

$$\nabla^2 u + \frac{\omega^2}{v^2} u = 0 \qquad \nabla^2 u + \frac{2m}{\hbar^2}(\hbar\omega - U)u = 0$$

write $\quad \omega u \sim -\dfrac{1}{i}\dfrac{\partial\psi}{\partial t}$

Time dependent Schrodinger equation

(3) $\quad \nabla^2\psi + \dfrac{2mi}{\hbar}\dfrac{\partial\psi}{\partial t} - \dfrac{2m}{\hbar^2}U\psi = 0$

Written also as

(4) $\quad i\hbar\dfrac{\partial\psi}{\partial t} = -\dfrac{\hbar^2}{2m}\nabla^2\psi + U\psi$

(Comments: ψ complex)

Time dep. equation (assuming (2))

(5) $\quad W\psi = -\dfrac{\hbar^2}{2m}\nabla^2\psi + U\psi$

Valid only for states of fixed energy $W = \hbar\omega$

Continuity equation for (4)
Write conjugate equation

(6) $\quad -i\hbar\dfrac{\partial\psi^*}{\partial t} = -\dfrac{\hbar^2}{2m}\nabla^2\psi^* + U\psi^*$

$(4) \times \psi^* - (6) \times \psi$ fields

(7) $\quad \dfrac{\partial}{\partial t}(\psi^*\psi) + \nabla\cdot\left\{\dfrac{\hbar}{2mi}\left(\psi^*\nabla\psi - \psi\nabla\psi^*\right)\right\}$

Suggested provisional interpretation

(8) $\quad \psi^*\psi = |\psi|^2 = $ density of probability

(9) $\quad \dfrac{\hbar}{2mi}\left(\psi^*\nabla\psi - \psi\nabla\psi^*\right) = $ average value of flow density

__Normalization :__   (8) suggests to determine ψ such that

(10) $\quad \int|\psi|^2 d\tau = \int\psi^*\psi\, d\tau = 1$

This requires certain conditions
a) Near singular pt ψ less ∞ than $r^{-3/2}$
b) Limit of infinite distance $\psi\to 0$ faster than $r^{-3/2}$

Exceptions to rule (6) will have to be considered later

__Generalizations.__
Point on line

(11) $\quad\begin{cases} i\hbar\dfrac{\partial\psi}{\partial t} = -\dfrac{\hbar^2}{2m}\dfrac{\partial^2\psi}{\partial t^2} + U(x)\psi \\[2mm] \text{or} \\[1mm] E\,u(x) = -\dfrac{\hbar^2}{2m}\dfrac{d^2u}{dx^2} + U(x)u \end{cases}$

Rotator with fixed axis
$A = $ mom. of inertia

(12) $\quad\begin{cases} i\hbar\dfrac{\partial\psi}{\partial t} = -\dfrac{\hbar^2}{2A}\dfrac{\partial^2\psi}{\partial\alpha^2} + U(\alpha)\,\psi(\alpha,t) \\[2mm] \text{or} \\[1mm] E\,u(\alpha) = -\dfrac{\hbar^2}{2A}\dfrac{d^2u}{d\alpha^2} + U(\alpha)\,u(\alpha) \end{cases}$

Point on sphere or dumbell with fixed c. of grav.

(13) $\quad \Lambda\psi = \dfrac{1}{\sin\vartheta}\dfrac{\partial}{\partial\vartheta}\left(\sin\vartheta\,\dfrac{\partial\psi}{\partial\vartheta}\right) + \dfrac{1}{\sin^2\vartheta}\dfrac{\partial^2\psi}{\partial\varphi^2}$

Notes on Quantum Mechanics, Enrico Fermi, 1954

COMPASSION AND SUBJECTIVITY

EXCERPT FROM A CONVERSATION
BETWEEN AMNON YARIV AND
ENRIQUE MARTINEZ CELAYA

Enrique Martínez Celaya: What do you think is the role of compassion in science?

Amnon Yariv: Compassion in science? I never thought of it. Give me some clues. Compassion for?

EMC: Wislawa Szymborska has said that in Poland poetry had to be an instrument of compassion because of everything around them after the war. Poetry had to be part of all the destruction, sadness, loss and confusion. This is a big issue for me in the arts and I was wondering if you have encountered it in science?

AY: You know, my answer would be no. I think science regards itself as dispassionate or independent of human conditions. Absolute truth is out there and it is our job to find it. It makes science absolutely objective. There is a great deal of subjectivity in how you attack it—what topics you choose to work on and what kind of methods you bring to bear. But I have never heard the word compassion used in the context of science.

Quiet Night (dirt) 1999 ▶

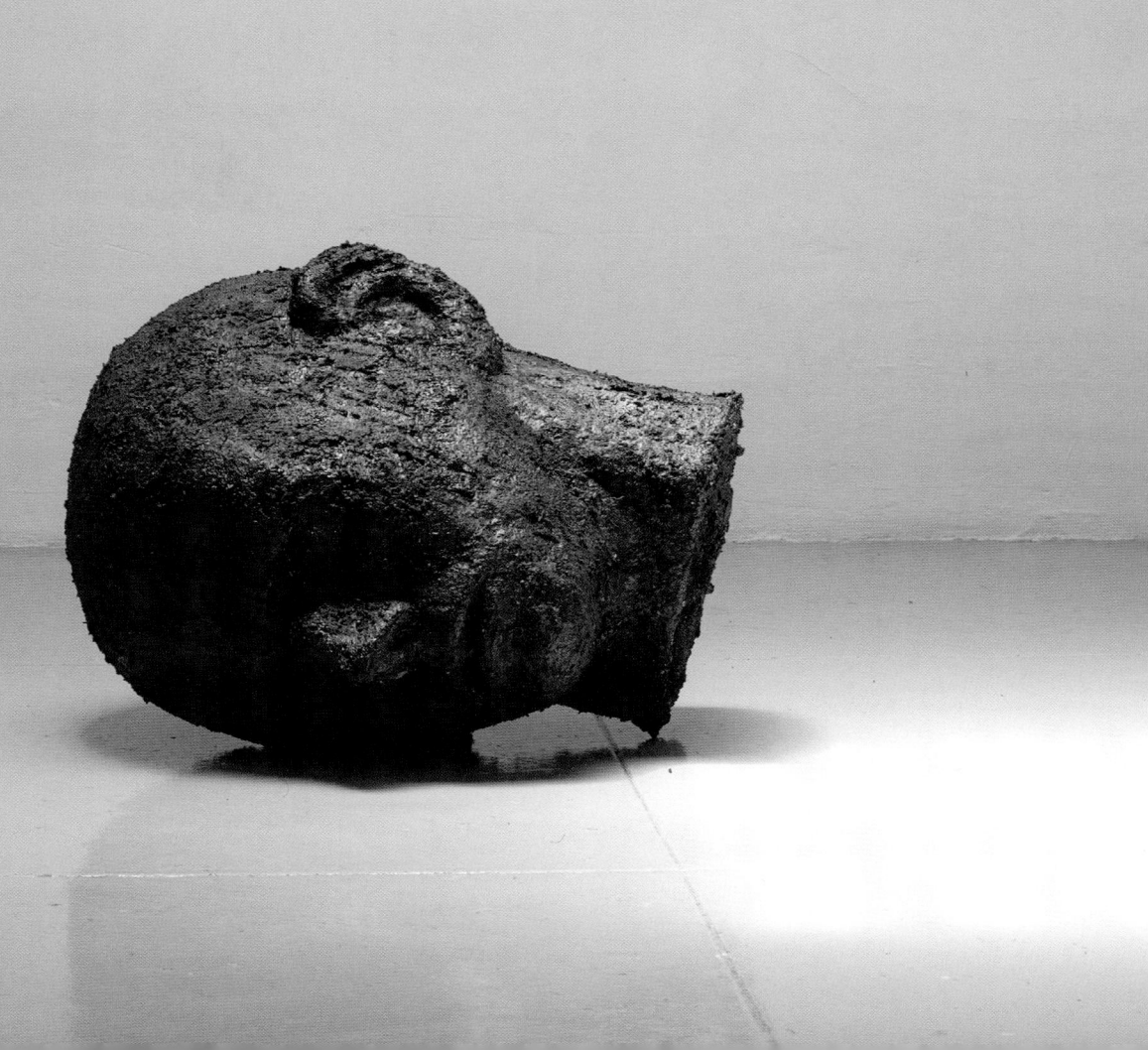

Szymborska justified Polish poetry taking the direction it did, because of need, social need. In a way she used poetry as a tool to achieve something. A tool can be bent, because once you have an aim in mind, then if the tool doesn't quite do it, you bend it so it can. But science is to us absolutely objective, as I said. And therefore, it's not a tool for anything. It is an aim by itself. It's truth. Because truth can be bent by morality or people, in science we say that everything eventually has to withstand experimentation. That is what truth is. If you can predict and then do experiments to verify, then you have a theory. So one can, maybe, sneak compassion into it, but it would be hard.

EMC: Do you think that scientists, are more or less likely to be compassionate than the average individual?

AY: I think that people who deal with ideas tend to be more compassionate and in general more socially aware. Maybe the science background enables them to look at the world more objectively and to peel off the lies. It makes them more analytical, more critical. So maybe... is that what you meant? I don't think that science itself is necessarily compassionate but I think many scientists are.

EMC: What is the future of science?

AY: I think the future of science looks good. There will always be science. Its popularity may wax and wane, but I think that from day one people have always been interested in the universe... tried to understand more and more, and that is really the basis for science. Science has acquired a little more power and prestige since the second World War just because of the fact that it helped America win the war... the A-bomb. But even before that and after that, what drives science is curiosity. And curiosity is part of human nature.

EMC: Do you have any particular questions in science that you would like to see answered? Special curiosities? Unfinished business?

AY: I think that the world was created by God to be infinite, and regardless of how much we learn, what we don't know will forever remain infinite. Which means there will be work forever for scientists. And you are not working as a physicist in order to get all the answers, you're working just to increase that which you know. So, yes, I have my agenda of things that I'm interested in, but there isn't something which I feel that I need to finish. If I die tomorrow it is okay. I have done something, taught a few people... good enough.

EMC: Sometimes when people ask me about my science background and its relationship to art, the question of faith and intuition comes up. In your scientific work is there room for faith or intuition?

AY: Most of us that are doing research are at the boundary between the known and unknown. And the boundary is kind of fuzzy. Everything here is known perfectly well, and from here on, not at all. There's that gray area in between. But you are roughly at the boundary. And that's what the search for definition is. And you have to make guesses. And the guesses are intuitive guesses, about what things are going on and what kind of experiments you are going to conduct. I think this boundary, although we keep pushing

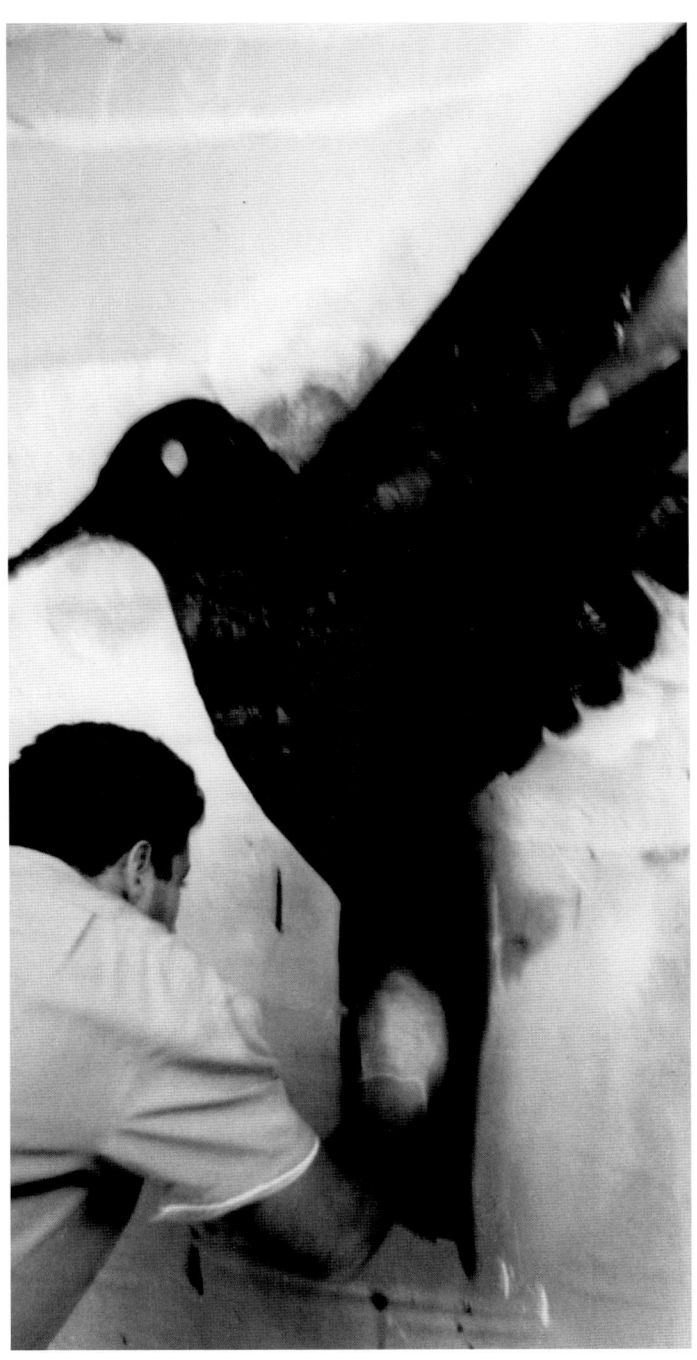

it, will never get to the end. The barrier between the known and the unknown is infinite. There will never be an end to it.

EMC: I like the mystery in this boundary between the known and the unknown. Despite the vastness of this infinite territory of the unknown one can make incursions or probes with imagination and insight. Intuition is not the only quality that relates science and art. When I talk about science and its relationship to art, questions of language and translation often come up.

AY: Language... you know, mathematics is the language of physics and I really don't think that you can convey it in any fashion short of learning it. That's why I think that laymen don't really understand science. Mathematics is one of the crowning pieces of human achievement and it is the language of physics. This is a difficulty and a disadvantage of science. People can appreciate the beauty in art. People can come to the museum and see your work but I can't describe what I do to my friends. The language, the consistency, the logic, the beauty of the language or experiences are not transferable.

EMC: Well if you think of this description as a translation, art is not so different. Most people do not understand or relate to contemporary art. You can describe what you're doing in physics but you can not actually do the physics at the level of description. You have to ultimately use the language of physics, mathematics and so on. Art is very similar in the sense that you can explain the issues that you understand in the work, you can explain some of your ideas and part of the context in which it is created, but

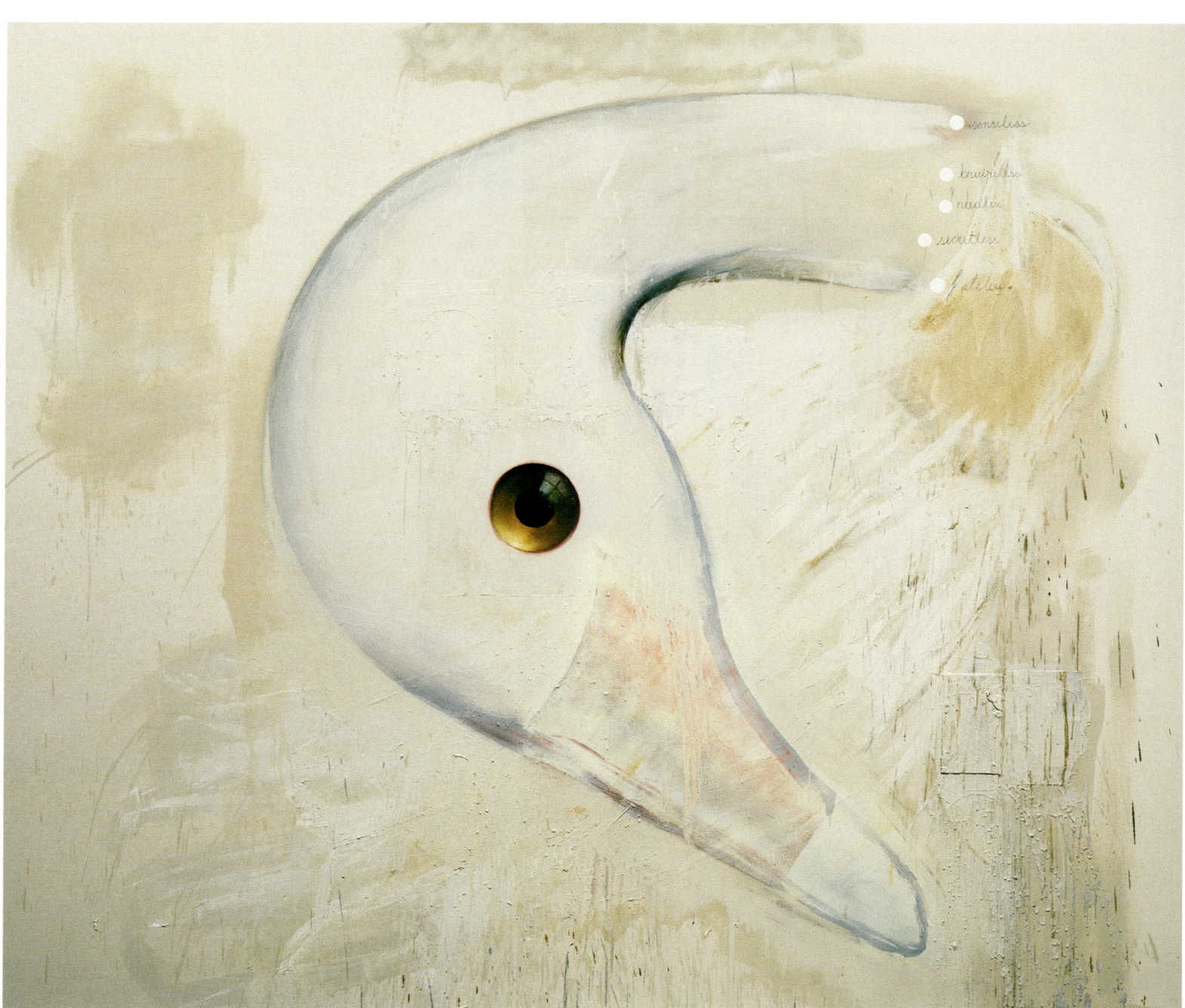

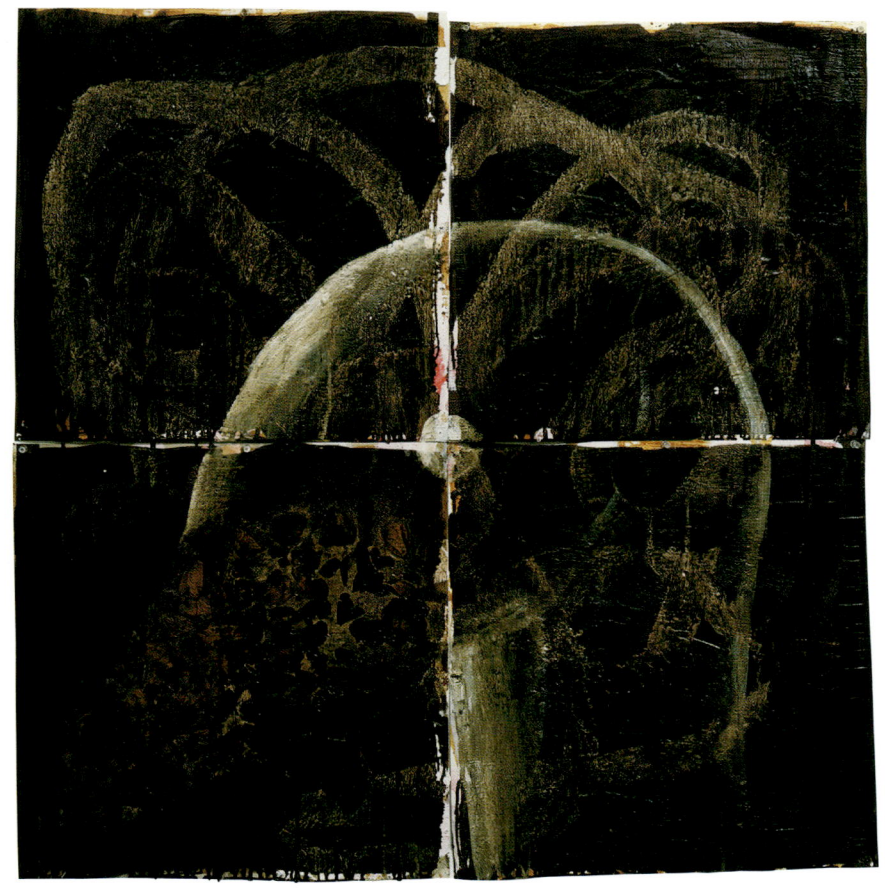

◀ Master Song 1999   Circumstances and Resolutions 1999

ultimately the meaning is embodied in the way it was made. And if you try to break it down and translate it you end up at the level of description similar to a physicist. You cannot make art at the level of that description. You can not make art by just the combination of interesting ideas that you may mention in a description.

AY: Well, art must be much more subjective. I mean, take physics. Take two professors who will teach, let's say, very advanced general relativity. One in the United States and one in China. They will essentially use the same language and say the same things more or less... convey the same picture. While two artists describing the same piece of art, will probably say very different things. There is a certain elemental objectivity to physics which, I guess, maybe doesn't exist in art, because it is so subjective.

EMC: I do not completely agree. In physics you test your calculation to see if the solution is right. By contrast, many are of the opinion that every position is equally valid in art and that "correctness" is not the issue, that there is no test. While subjectivity is intrinsic to the choices of artists and viewers, it is not the whole picture. You see a tree painted by Mondrian and a tree painted by Leonardo. The embodiment of the idea is very different. Very different trees. But when people describe how these trees evoke feeling and thoughts they will say very similar things. It is true that describing your preference for a visual experience is an aspect of subjectivity. But two well painted trees seem to often speak similarly to their audience despite descriptive differences. Of course, what I am making here is a simple argument for essence. What physicists might describe as the basis of nature. Maybe it is something hard to name without naming those parts that you can see on

the outside, but there is something they are all going around. Does that make sense?

AY: It sounds a little strange. Because as a physicist, you talk about this common core, but I really do not know what it is and I am not convinced that it does exist. I know you could not prove it exists, and that is why it is art and not physics. I thought until I spoke to you that art really was much more intuitive and subjective. I think, in my opinion, that trying to find maybe a common utopia, a logical element in art the same way that you do in physics is maybe trying to force an artificial constraint on art. It may not be necessary. I mean you know, probably, that most artists don't ask these questions ever, right? Something is pushing them. They are driven by something which probably they cannot express.

EMC: I do not think that many interesting contemporary artists ignore these questions. I believe in the clarity and power of emotional insight as a component of the work. But I also believe in a certain amount of other factors involved. The landscape of contemporary art has changed significantly and many simply detest the idea of the artist working from inspirational effort devoid of reflective insight. Being conscious of what you're trying to do does not strip away the emotion, validity, or directness of it.

AY: But probably there are many different ways of telling stories which are all equally valid.

EMC : That is the question, whether they *are* all equally valid. Ultimately what makes an approach valid is whether it leads to a good work.

AY: By moving other people. By making them feel something.

EMC: Right. A painting is its own argument, a defense of its own validity.

AY: Suppose you painted a work about your grandfather, the relationship you had, his love for animals, birds. The audience may just see a picture of an old man feeding a bird and some of them will be moved, but maybe not for the same reasons that moved you to paint it.

EMC: Right. But it is the same as in any other field. You might construct something and the knowledge and information used to construct it does not show. The object can be opaque to information about its motivations. As long as the object works, maybe it does not matter.

I need full investment in the elements involved in order to make the works meaningful to me. It helps me get up every day and work. It also helps to strip away the inconsequential issues. It is not uncommon for me to paint a dozen times over a painting.

AY: You go over it and start again?

EMC: Yes. I start again or cover parts. Sometimes a visitor comes to my studio and likes a painting and then two weeks later they call me about it but the painting no longer exist because it didn't survive.

AY: It didn't pass your test of authenticity, of being real. Well maybe what you sense then is its truth. But you could have painted your grandfather on a different day when the sun was not sunny but cloudy and you had just

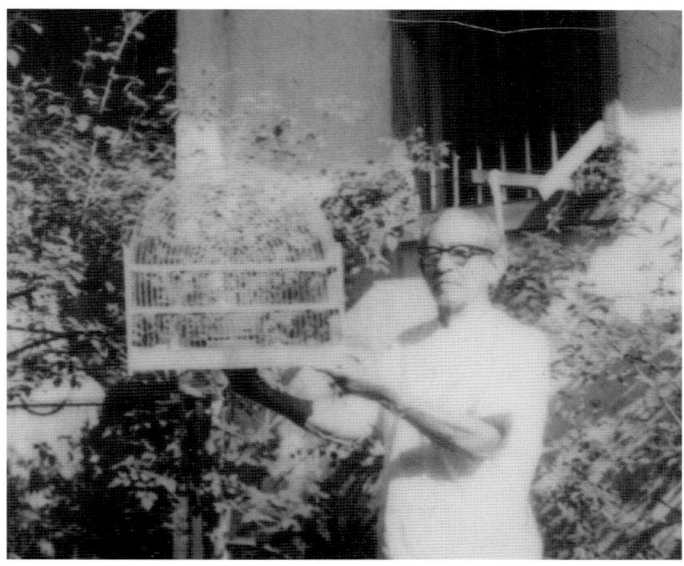

Tomás Celaya, Palos, Cuba

watched an accident in the street, so you would have been in a completely different mood and because of that would have painted different paintings—still truthful. You would have wound up with a different painting which would have passed your own test possibly.

EMC: Possibly. But most likely those two or three different kinds of paintings, all of which passed the test, share a large number of constants and I think that is the issue for me. I think there are some things that remain constant and you can always recognize them in the work of an artist. Not only because of a certain look, but because of a specific sensibility and the choice of certain parameters. So much of art is also what you leave out and choose not to include, the kind of economy you use.

Overleaf
Black Flower 1999 ▶

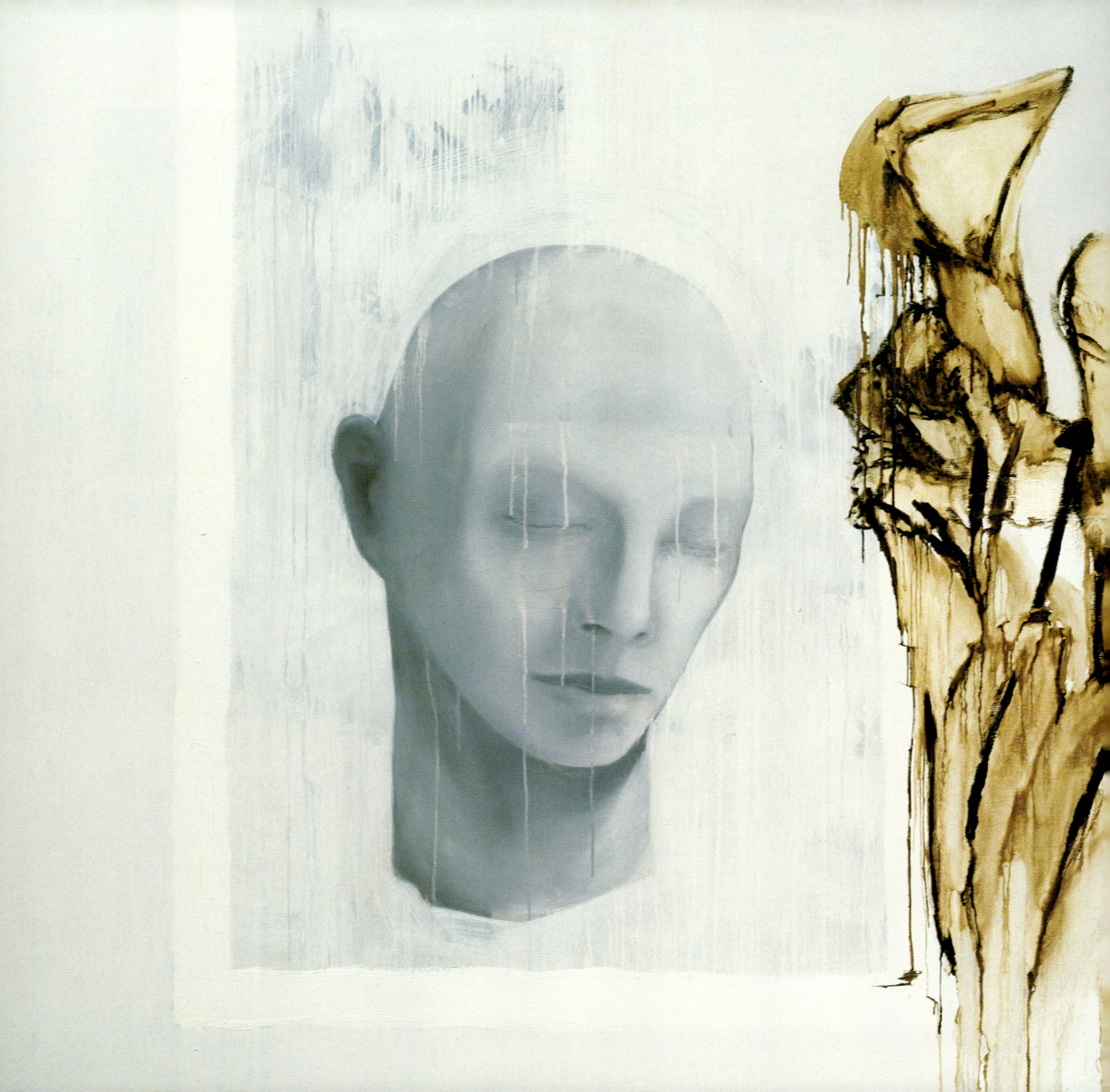

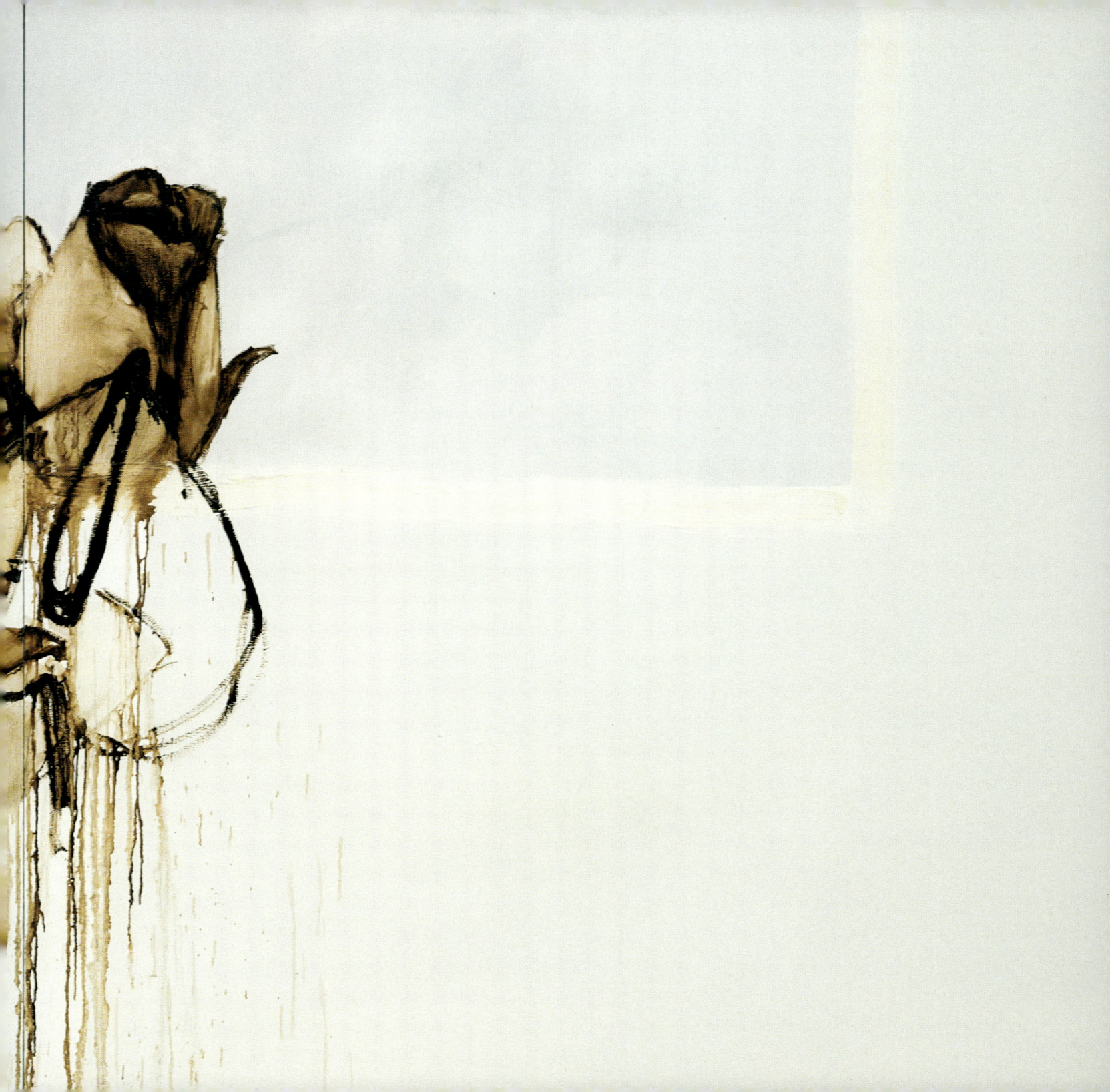

IMAGERY AND PROCESS

EXCERPT FROM A CONVERSATION
BETWEEN DONALD BAECHLER AND
ENRIQUE MARTINEZ CELAYA

David Minnery: Thinking about this dialogue has brought up many questions about both of your work. Perhaps we can start with the sources for the work. What sources do you use?

Donald Baechler: What sources don't I use would be a better question. They seem to come from all over the place. They come from a general kind of feeling of nostalgia from childhood and they come from advertising and they come from art of the insane and children's art. Every sort of image that sticks to me as I move through the world ends up somehow informing what I'm doing in the paintings.

Enrique Martinez Celaya: And you collect them on your travels also.

DB: Yes, I'm always coming back with suitcases and boxes full of things. And maybe about one half of one percent of it actually ends up being used.

EMC: For me, the sources for the images can derive from

childhood, the everyday, nature, and literature. They are usually very simple images. They are very accessible as things you will recognize immediately. Not usually from culture.

DB: Popular culture?

EMC: Right. I do not mine popular culture for imagery.

DB: You use literature though, that is interesting.

EMC: Literature is an important part of the work. Poetry in particular, but literature in general. And a lot of the people that I think about are people in literature.

DB: Really? Like who?

EMC: Paul Celan and Herman Melville for example.

DM: Donald, do you find that writing or literature plays any role in informing your work?

DB: That is an interesting question. It is something I haven't given much thought to, but I don't ever really consciously refer to, or somehow I've never been able to draw literature into the visual sphere of what I'm doing.

•••

DM: Both you and Enrique have used images of heads, birds, and flowers in your work. How do you address these images, particularly in regard to their almost trite familiarity?

DB: I think the word trite is a horrible word. I think it is a pejorative term and I would never use it in relation to anything I'm doing, or with what Enrique is doing either, certainly. I know what you mean, but I think it is a bad choice of words. But I think that, for me, the head is almost always a kind of surrogate for a self portrait, and the flowers almost a replacement for the human figure in the painting. I've made an almost intentional point of not studying botany or not learning what these flowers are that I'm drawing. I buy flowers at the Korean deli on the corner, but you know, I can barely distinguish between a tulip and a rose, which sounds stupid, but it's true. For me a flower has this very convenient, almost human dimension, with the head and the stem and the leaves replacing certain body parts. I think Enrique may have a more emotional attachment to flowers than I do. They seem in your work to provoke a kind of memory or sense of loss.

EMC: I really like what you just said about the idea of surrogates for the human figure. I think that is a very useful way of thinking. Heads and flowers are overused, and I am interested in the sort of overload and erosion of these images with overuse. I try to recontextualize them and obtain a simultaneous friction between their familiarity and their new context. Also I often think of flowers, especially tulips, as symbols of decay and fungus.

DB: Really. Tulips make you think of decay?

EMC: They are padded and they have a skin-like feeling, somewhat morbid and associated with wealth.

DB: The whole Dutch thing. I have read a lot of

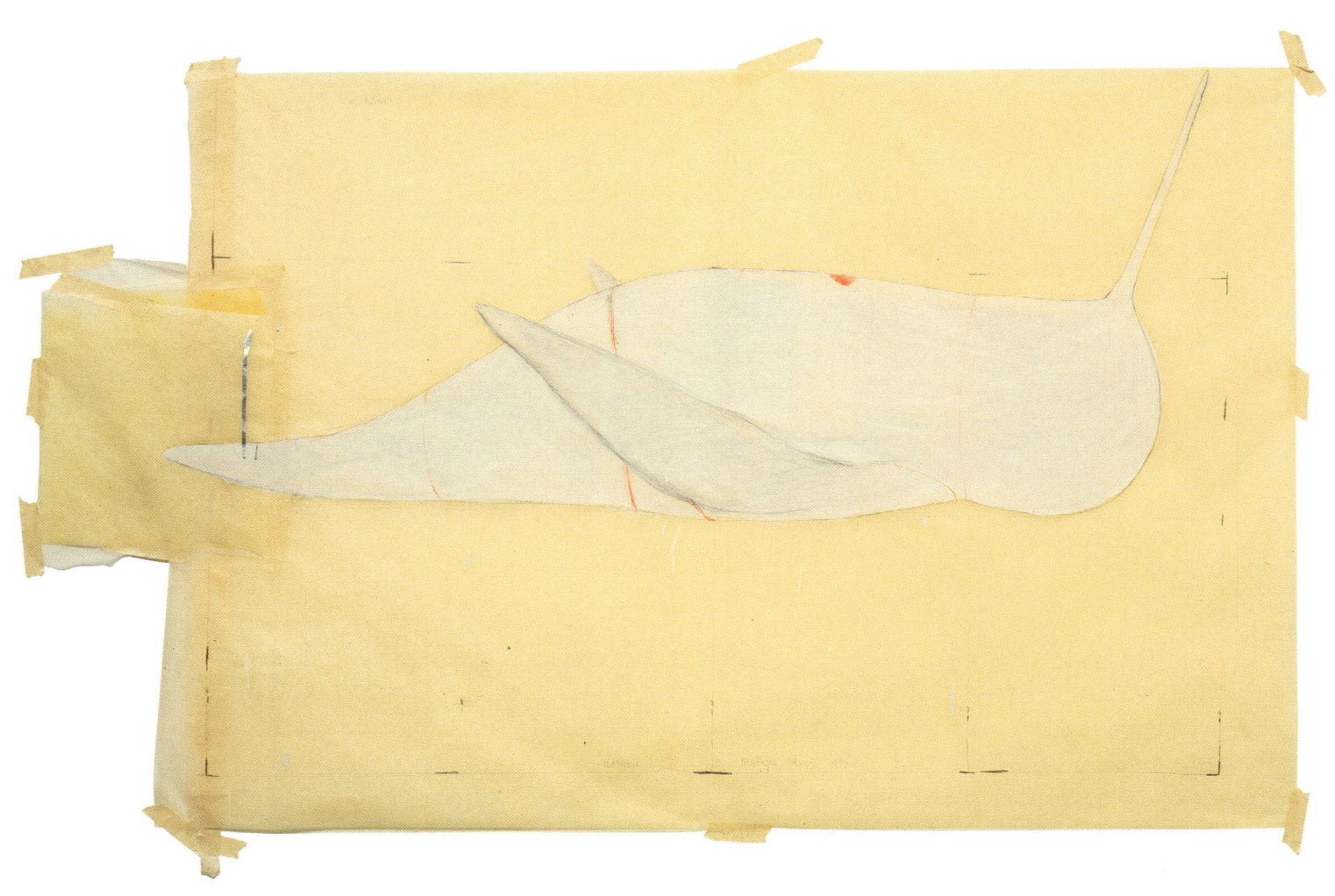

Acceptance of Longing (study) 1997

anecdotes about the Dutch tulip economy. The relationship between flowers and economics is fascinating. It is actually kind of unexpected and really hard to imagine. I mean it's hard to imagine it repeating itself in any sense.

EMC: In some cases, the painters would continue to add flowers to a painting as the patron acquired new tulip bulbs. Sort of an ongoing painting.

•••

DM: Do you find that your paintings bring about a sense of melancholy?

DB: I think they do, but I think other people don't think they do. People often end up thinking my paintings are comical in some sense, but in general I'm a melancholic person. Maybe I'm just missing the point of my own paintings, but I believe that I'm conveying some sense of melancholy. Some people agree with me, some people don't.

EMC: I think of your paintings back in the eighties with figures and the suggestion of the landscape. Those were powerful and melancholic and almost had a Caspar David Friedrich feeling to them. Not only in the obvious part of the landscape but in the sense of largeness about them.

DB: I know what you are talking about. Yes, I was interested in Caspar David Friedrich and the Hudson River School—the figure isolated in the landscape, the figure alone in the world. But then at a certain point I started to want to fill things up a bit more and crowd things in a lot more. So maybe that sense of melancholy went out the

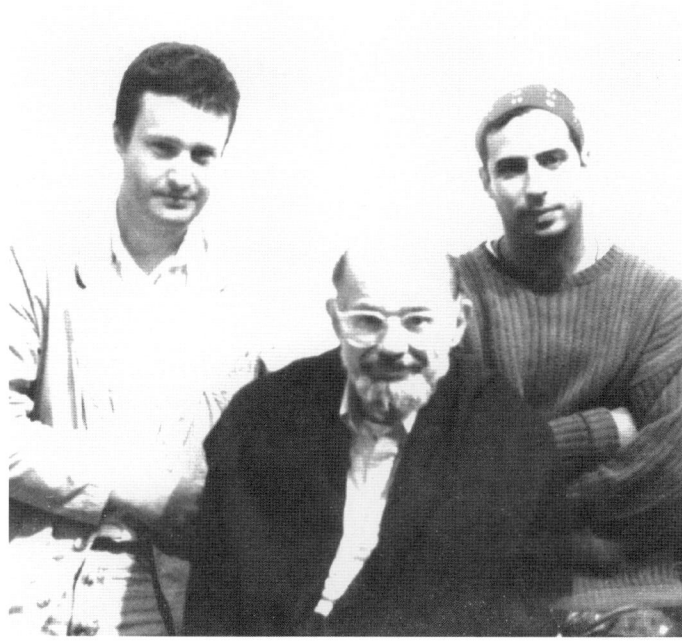

Donald Baechler, Allen Ginsberg and Enrique Martínez Celaya, 1994

window with the empty fields. I don't know. Enrique, your paintings certainly seem melancholic in their use of black and the kind of poetic line that you employ.

EMC: The problem with the character of melancholia is that it can completely override a painting. It can completely undermine it, so I try to keep melancholia and nostalgia at bay. I think that is where they are most subversive, most interesting.

DB: Hopefully kept at bay. Melancholia evokes awful emotions actually. Awful sentiments in some sense.

EMC: Right. But pitting a certain amount of rigidity against melancholia somehow creates an interesting struggle within the painting and refreshes a painting constantly. Paintings that are deliberately serious are often very predictable. I like to find seriousness in unexpected places.

DB: I have an attraction to melancholia and also to a kind of ridiculousness and absurdity. I like to mix the comic and the serious into one sort of big soup. I don't know if it works or not, but I think sometimes it does.

EMC: I think it works. I think it works in your paintings.

• • •

DM: The work of both of you contains figurative and non-figurative elements. With regard to the surface of your paintings and the images you use, do you find there's a tension between the imagery and the surface of the painting?

DB: I hope so. I construct the sort of surface that I paint on—that I've been painting on for the last ten years or so—to intentionally deflect the line and prevent the line from being too perfect. There is this dialogue going on between two different types of painted elements. One of which characteristically would be the kind of heavy black line and then something naturalistically painted like a vegetable or some sort of species of post-supremacist abstraction. A kind of dialogue between two different types of line making or image making in the same painting. In the past I have said that it represents man's uneasy relationship to abstraction and to the natural world. For me it is a simple desire to kind of churn things up a little.

EMC: In your surfaces, you have materials put on them such as fabrics and erasures. Are those part of the con-

structing process of the paintings or are they premeditated?

DB: Some of it is premeditated, some of it is part of the painting. Certainly in my case what you see on the canvas is never how the painting began. There is a lot of doubt and a lot of change that goes on in the process. But there is also this false archeology that I construct to begin with by layering on all this crap on the canvas before I even start painting on it. For me that's just preparing a ground. But then on top of that there is this other sort of history going on with erasure and change and doubt.

EMC: I think we share many ideas but I think I have a more troubled relationship with surface and marks. I end up with complex surfaces by pasting stuff, painting over parts as I am trying to get to a better painting. I am willing to sacrifice anything for a painting that will be moving. I do not try to make an interesting painting. I am trying to make a painting that is resonant, and because of that, I end up destroying a lot of work, and the surfaces accumulate some of that history.

DB: Destroy a lot of work? You mean you actually destroy them, or you just paint on top of them?

EMC: I do both but I was referring to painting on top of them. But I do have an uneasy relationship with all the signifiers or all the things that reference emotion like erasures or transparencies or drips. They only survive in the paintings after a lot of internal reconciliation.

DB: I think that's clear in your paintings. There is nothing that looks false in those paintings. I know exactly what you mean. I think maybe that's the difference between a good painting and a bad painting, it is that level of conviction with which the painter can bring, just exactly, what you call signifiers. It's easy to drip and it's easy to scribble something out, but it's really hard to do it in a way that means anything.

•••

DM: How do you know when a work is finished?

DB: I think DeKooning answered this question once on a radio interview, he said something like, at some point I just paint myself right out of the painting. I feel that. Certainly there are artists whom I admire greatly like Peter Halley who I think goes from point A to point B and then to point C and then he is finished because it was mapped out before he started painting. But for me, and I think maybe for Enrique also, the painting evolves in an intuitive way and just at some point, there it is. It's done.

EMC: My feeling about finishing work is similar to yours. I think there is a moment in which a painting feels perfect, and it usually has to do with the moment in which the painting seems truly moving, direct and unencumbered with stuff that is not necessary. I do not usually say intuition but it is a good way to describe it. The painting seems to connect to paintings that I respect and love.

DB: Are you saying that sometimes in your own paintings you experience something that's equivalent to other paintings that you know?

EMC: Yes. An equivalent feeling, not a familiar look.

DB: That's interesting, because I think sometimes that pops into my work as well.

EMC: I have this repertoire of paintings and painters that I think about like Giorgione and I think of what emerges out of those paintings. I am not interested in copies nor mannerisms and I have different preocupations than those whom I admire, but I pursue some of the feelings that are in those great paintings. Sometimes that feeling comes from a great writer like Melville.

DB: I only think of Melville as maybe the quintessential American novelist and it's interesting that you're attached to him.

EMC: I am very interested in American literature and American art. There is something about Americans which I didn't understand before I lived in this country. Americans have a distance that is very necessary to them for surviving with their artwork. They need to create it and then fight against it and there is a no-nonsense quality to it that I enjoy. Take John Singleton Copley and compare him to the English painters of the same period. Their work had fuzzy landscapes and then suddenly you see Copley and you see his paintings having this beautiful direct sharpness. There is no fuzziness, but a balance with nature, an ascetic romanticism. This is true of American literature also. There is, of course, Russian, German, Spanish, and Latin American literature which is beautiful, strong and clear but there is something about the American tradition that I really like. It feels simultaneously familiar and foreign.

David Minnery is a sculptor currently living in Los Angeles

White island / black sea

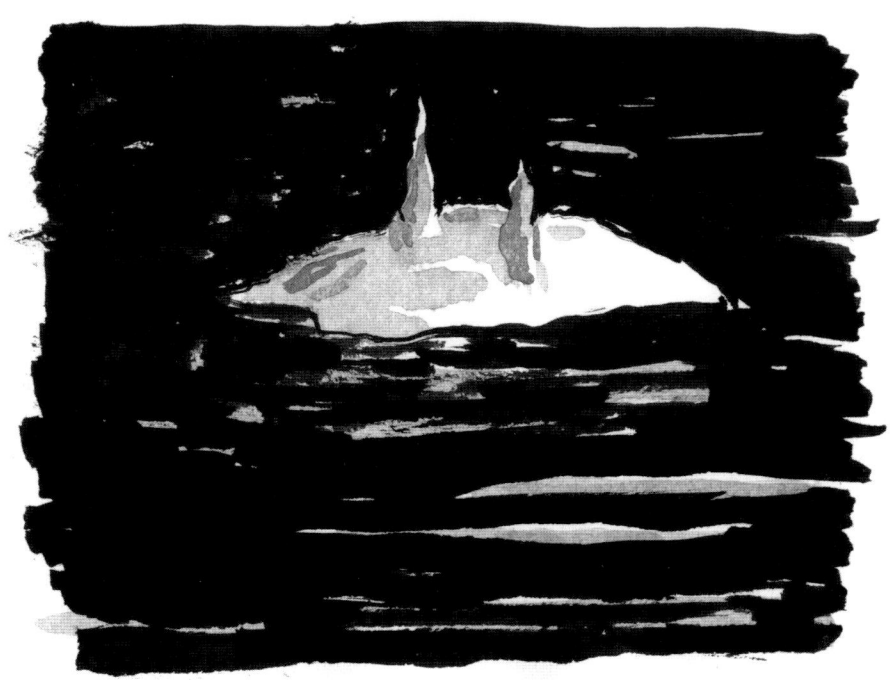

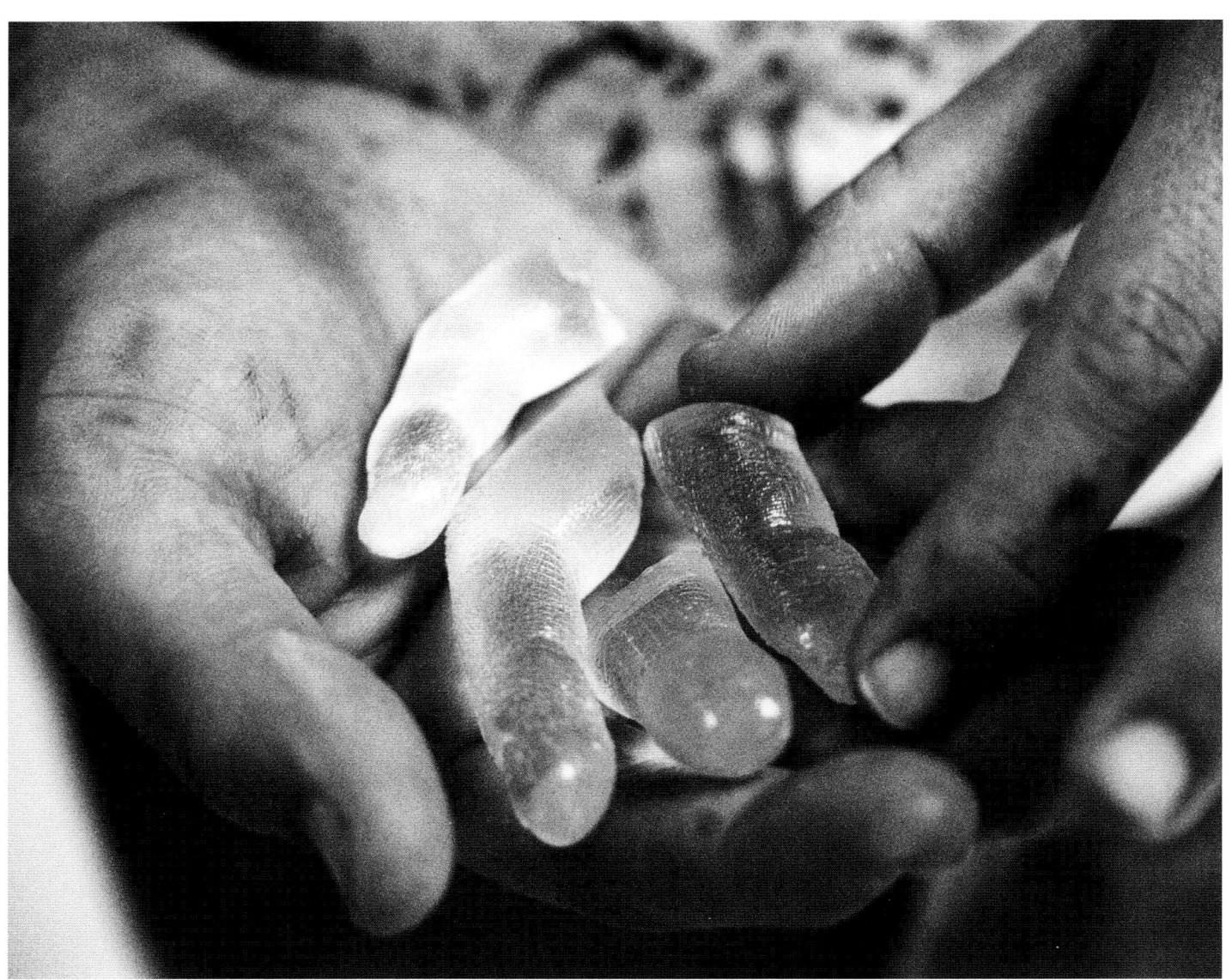

Thoughts on beauty

— beauty as presented in art is
often related to visual delectation.
I do see it that way.

Instead I propose the following
leads to the nature of beauty

— moving or arousing first ⟹ (could)
    to beauty   leads

— elegance — not the same but could lead
    to experience of beauty

— efficiency

— clarity↲

⟶ But if I'm not the same,
the next question is "who in the world
        am I" — L.C

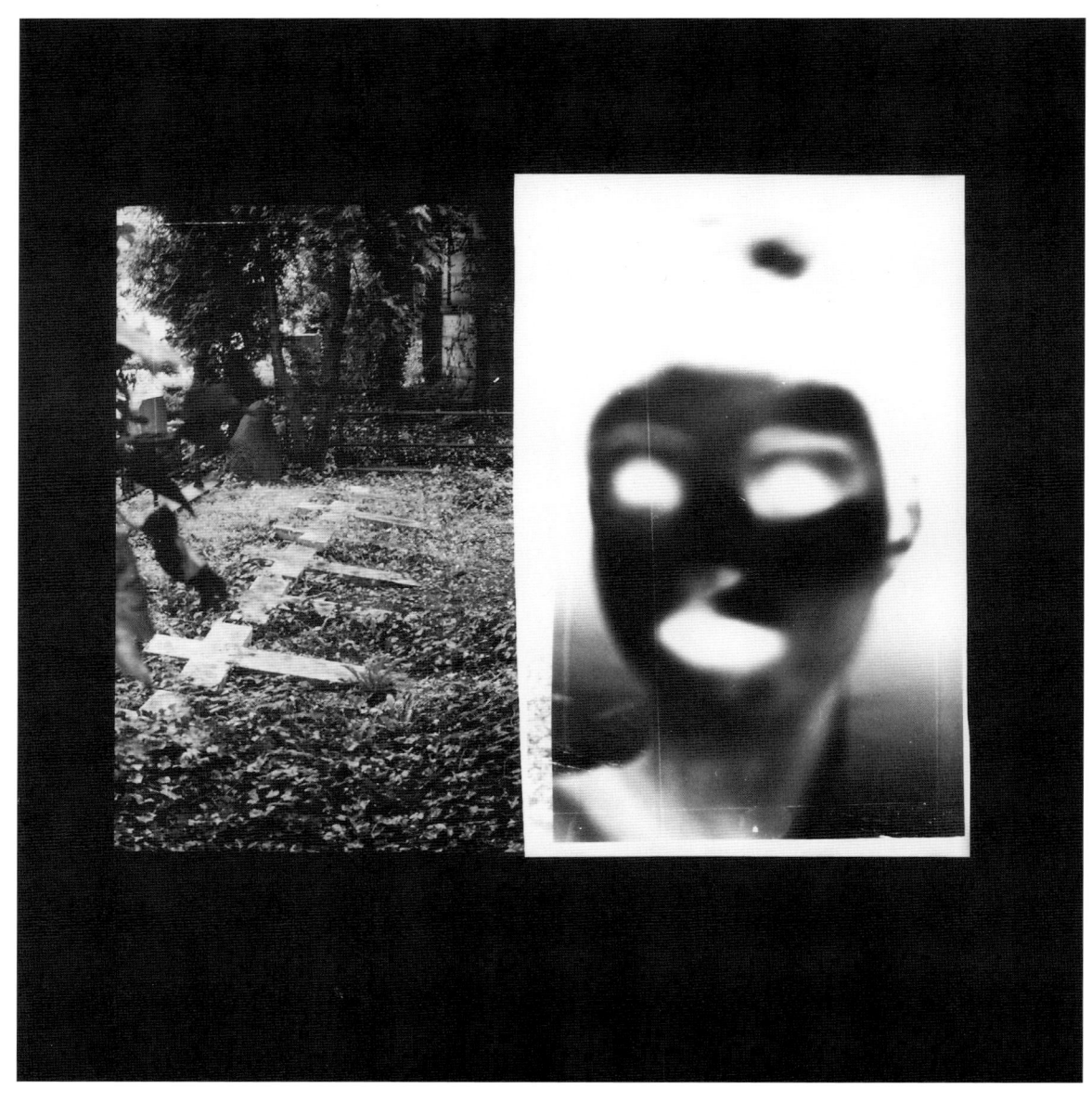

The warden 1998
The Museum of Fine Arts, Houston

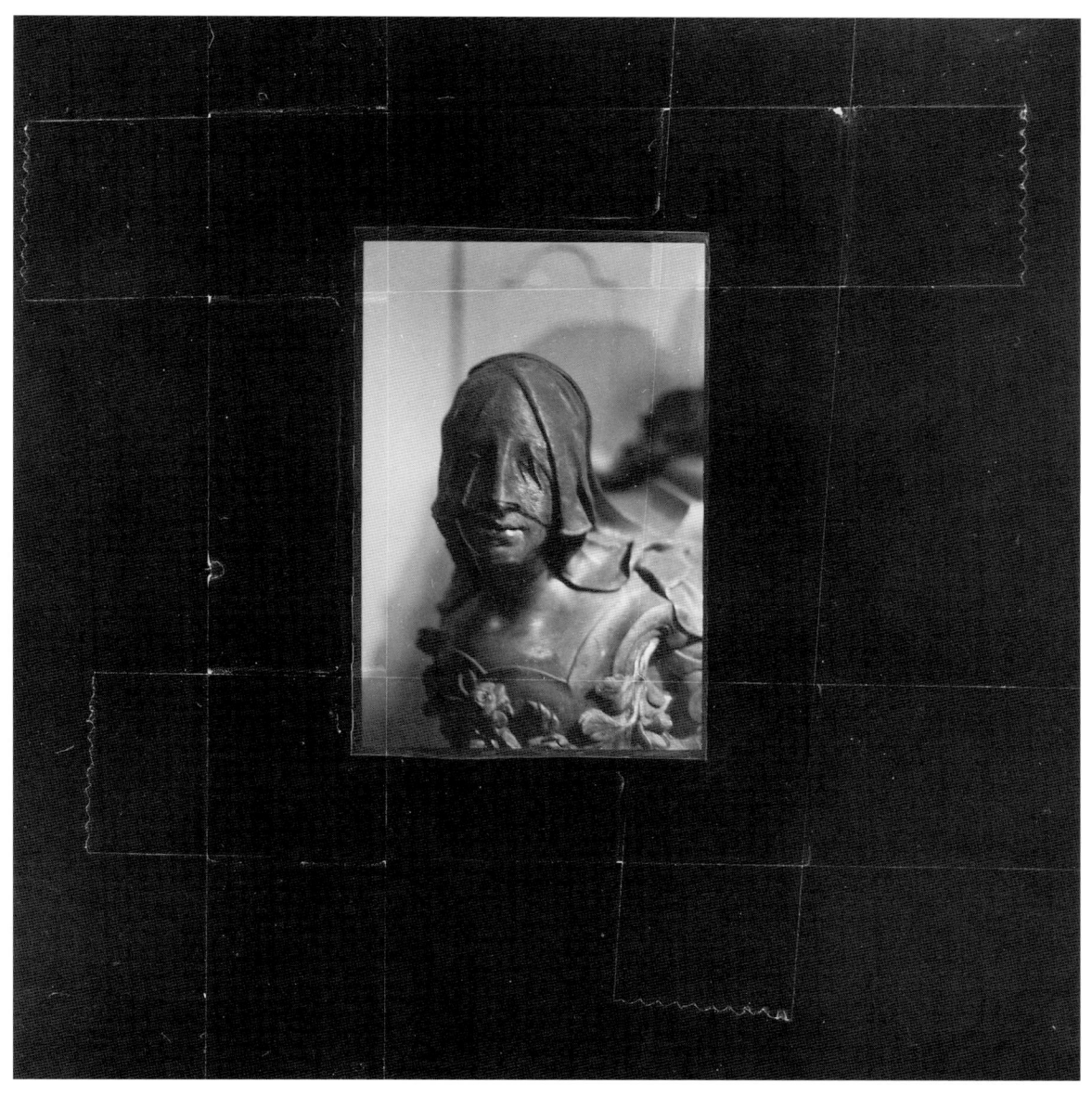

The size of a wound 1998

p. 11
The Trouble with Memory 1993
Oil, wax and silk flowers on canvas
78 x 66 in., 198 x 168 cm

p. 15
No Doubt Good Writing 1995
Charcoal and collage on paper
17 x 16 in., 43 x 41 cm

p. 18
The Right Word 1995
Oil and wax on canvas
72 x 60 in., 183 x 152 cm

p. 19
The Liar and the Thief 1996
Enamel and oil on canvas
72 x 60 in., 183 x 152 cm

p. 23
The River 1997
Oil on wax and plaster
70 x 22 x 11 in., 178 x 56 x 28 cm

p. 24
Winter and silk flowers 1998
Gelatin silver print
16 x 16 in., 41 x 41 cm

p. 27
The Burden of Your Hand 1997
Oil on nylon
80 x 66 in., 203 x 168 cm

p. 31
Feeder and Voice 1999
Oil on waxed paper
52 x 52 in., 132 x 132 cm

p. 33
Acceptance of Longing 1997
Oil on canvas
66 x 72 in., 168 x 183 cm

p. 34
Tu Brazo (your arm) 1997
Enamel and oil on paper
18 x 48 in., 46 x 122 cm

p. 35
Vanity and Redemption 1997
Oil on canvas
54 x 60 in., 137 x 152 cm

p. 37
Stonewall 1997
Oil on assembled paper
75 x 39 in., 191 x 99 cm

p. 39
A boy in his room 1997
Oil on paper
24 x 18 in., 61 x 46 cm

The Secrets 1997
Oil on paper
24 x 18 in., 61 x 46 cm

p. 40
St. Catherine (Absolution) 1997
Resin
7 x 9 x 9 in., 18 x 23 x 23 cm

p. 41
The most fragile 1998
Watercolor and oil on paper
20 x 20 in., 51 x 51 cm

p. 42
First War 1998
Oil on paper
51.5 x 61 in., 131 x 156 cm

p. 43
Marker 1997
Plastic teeth in resin
4 x 21 x 4 in., 10 x 53 x 10 cm

p. 44
Quiet Night (recollection) I 1999
Oil on canvas
103 x 113 in., 262 x 287 cm

p. 45
Quiet Night (recollection) II 1999
Oil on canvas
103 x 113 in., 262 x 287 cm

p. 46
A Neck in Ashes 1997
Oil on paper
30 x 80 in., 76 x 203 cm

p. 47
Half Again, Flower 1998
Dirt, flowers and resin
6 x 8 x 9 in., 15 x 20 x 23 cm

p. 49
Black Hummingbird, White Birch 1999
Oil and tar on canvas
54 x 60 in., 137 x 152 cm

p. 51
The Undeniable and Unfortunate Truths
1998. Oil and graphite on canvas
96 x 88 in., 244 x 224 cm

p. 52-53
A Dry Bed 1998
Ink and graphite on paper
10 works, each 13 x 11 in., 33 x 28 cm

p. 55
Pena 1999
Oil, tar and objects on canvas
84 x 100 in., 213 x 254 cm

p. 56
Skin for the Morning I 1999
Watercolor on paper
13 x 11 in., 33 x 28 cm

p. 57
Skin for the Morning II, III, IV, V 1999
Watercolor on paper
13 x 11 in., 33 x 28 cm

p. 58
Quiet Night (wind) II, V 1999
Watercolor on paper
13 x 11 in., 33 x 28 cm

p. 59
Quiet Night (wind) III 1999
Watercolor on paper
13 x 10 in., 33 x 25 cm

p. 61
Open Sky, the Feeder 1999
Oil on canvas
66 x 72 in., 168 x 183 cm

p. 62
The Fall, Absolution 1999
Oil and petals on canvas
66 x 72 in., 168 x 183 cm

p. 63
Unbroken Poetry 1999
Oil, tar, feathers and fabric on canvas
94 x 94 in., 239 x 239 cm

pp. 64-65
The Field 1999
Oil and petals on canvas
84 x 100 in., 213 x 254 cm

p. 69
Quiet Night (dirt) 1999
Dirt, fiberglass and resin
25 x 34 x 30 in., 63 x 86 x 76 cm

p. 72
Master Song 1999
Oil, tar and graphite on canvas
84 x 100 in., 213 x 254 cm

p. 73
Circumstances and Resolutions 1999
Tar, oil and petals on paper
41 x 40 in., 104 x 102 cm

pp. 76-77
Black Flower 1999
Oil on canvas
66 x 144 in., 168 x 366 cm

p. 80
Acceptance of Longing (study) 1997
Oil on paper
36 x 60 in., 91 x 152 cm

p. 88
The warden
Gelatin silver print
16 x 16 in., 41 x 41 cm

p. 89
The size of a wound 1998
Gelatin silver print
16 x 16 in., 41 x 41 cm

p. 97
Circumstance (in progress) 1997
Oil on canvas
84 x 96 in., 213 x 244 cm

pp. 98-99
Quiet Night (ocean), Quiet Night
(marks) and Quiet Night (dirt) in the
artist studio.
Dirt, fiberglass and resin

p. 107
Quiet Night (ocean), performance view at
Marina del Rey, California, 1999
Gelatin silver print

p. 109
The great wait 1998
Photogravure on paper
7 x 7 in., 18 x 18 cm

p. 111
Leonardo 1999
Watercolor on paper
13 x 11 in., 33 x 28 cm

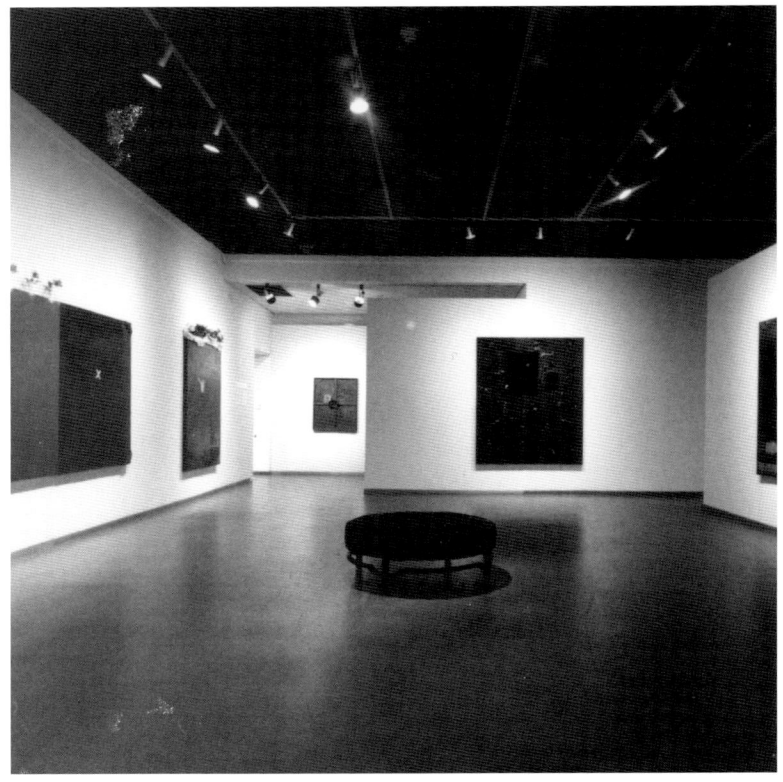

The Black Paintings at the University Art Museum, Santa Barbara, 1994

CHRONOLOGY/BIBLIOGRAPY

EDUCATION

CHRONOLOGY

EXHIBTION HISTORY

GENERAL REFERENCE ARTICLES AND INTERVIEWS

BOOKS, ARTIST'S PUBLICATIONS AND SOLO EXHIBITIONS CATALOGS

SELECTED PUBLIC COLLECTIONS

Education

University of California, M.F.A., Santa Barbara, 1994

Skowhegan School of Painting and Sculpture, Skowhegan, 1994

University of California, M.S., Berkeley, 1986-1988

Cornell University, B.S. with Distinction, Ithaca, 1982-1986

Liga de Arte de San Juan, San Juan, 1978-1980

Chronology

1964 - 1971

Born June 9, 1964, in Palos, Cuba, six years after the Cuban Revolution. First child of Marcos Enrique Fernando Martínez Rodriquez and Edilia Maximina Celaya Venereo. Shows intellectual promise from an early age. Regularly entertains patients with his singing in grandfather's dentist office. Learns archery and begins drawing. Father leaves for Spain in 1970.

1972 - 1974

Emigrates with mother and brother, Carlos, to Madrid. Family faced with financial difficulties. Has problems in school, turns to drawing. Attends three different schools in two years. Finds identification in drawing. Third brother,

Fernando, born in 1973. Takes first job collecting papers to sell to recyclers.

1975 - 1981

Moves to Puerto Rico with his family. At eleven, begins a traditional apprenticeship with painter Bartoldo Mayol and studies at the Liga de Arte de San Juan. At thirteen, writes four essays on Nietzsche, religion and adolescence, two are published. Continues painting, shows preference for oils and acrylics. Valedictorian of high school class. Article on his research with lasers is published in the Department of Energy magazine, after winning eight science competitions.

1982 - 1987

Studies Physics at Cornell University in Ithaca, New York. Graduates Magna Cum Laude in 1986. Begins his Ph.D. in Quantum Electronics at the University of California at Berkeley. Works at Brookhaven National Laboratory and publishes two physics papers. Paints during his summers on Long Island.

1988 - 1991

Switches in 1988 to graduate art program at Berkeley. Eight months later leaves school to work at a studio in Oakland. Supports himself by working for Coherent Medical, a laser company, where he patents four inventions. Dissatisfied in corporate environment, leaves Coherent. Supports himself by selling his art work in the parks of San Francisco and modeling (fashion). Travels to Europe and Africa with Brian Mountford. Publishes two works, *Guthrie* (Albee Press, Berkeley, 1989) and *Poems for the Bed* (Albee Press, Berkeley, 1991).

1992

First solo exhibition, mostly figurative works. Enrolls at the University of California at Santa Barbara. Receives two prestigious fellowships. Studies with Harry Reese with

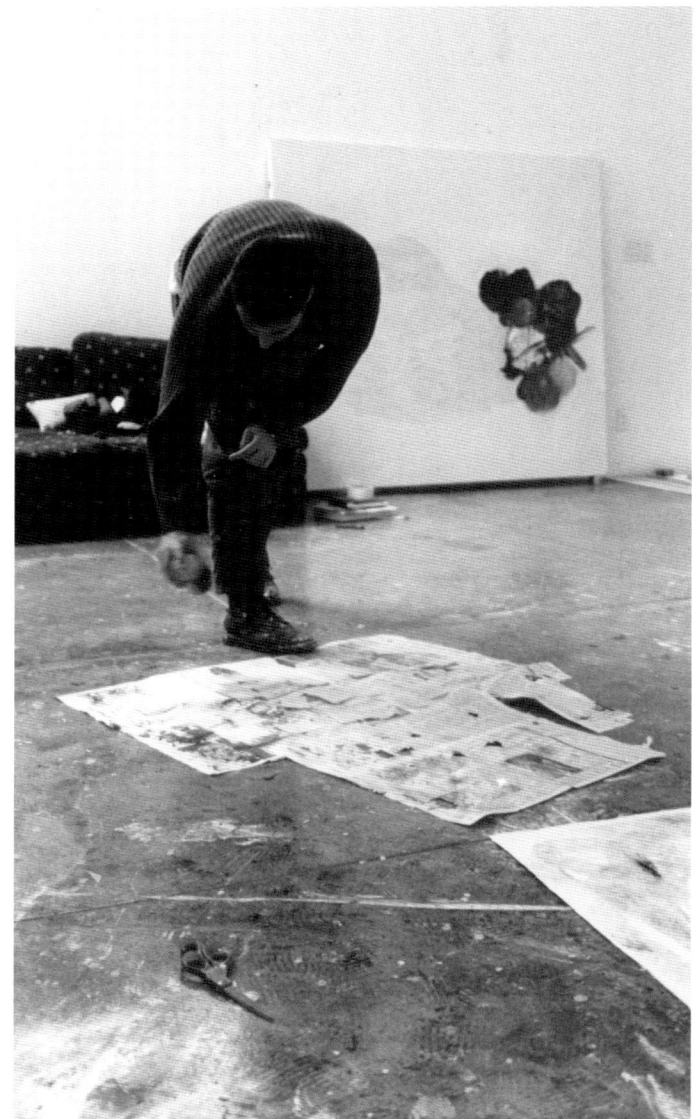

whom he shares an interest in poetry. Two professors that he studied with while at Berkeley, Joan Brown and Silvia Lark, pass away.

1993

Experiments with fabrics and materials. Removes figures from the paintings and destroys many of his earlier works. Exhibits in Puerto Rico. Several museums take interest in his work. Reads the poet Paul Celan for the first time.

1994

Receives M.F.A. from the University of California at Santa Barbara. Recipient of the University's highest honors: the Art Affiliates Award and Regents Fellowship. M.F.A. exhibition censored. Studies at the Skowhegan School of Painting and Sculpture, in Maine. Meets Donald Baechler and Allen Ginsberg. Opens three exhibits of the Black Paintings. Joins faculty at Pomona College in Claremont, California. Befriends the Ben Shahn art historian Frances Pohl. Moves to Pomona and takes an old newspaper pressroom next to a church as his studio.

1995

Is invited to join Dorothy Goldeen Gallery. Produces white paintings for first exhibition. Is included in several museum exhibitions. Spends time in New York with artists Donald Baechler and Pamela Fraser. Starts to write poems to be included in his exhibitions, and works with paint on paper. Spends time in London and researches Joan of Arc. Becomes increasingly interested in Zen philosophy and art that is simply articulated and serious.

1996

First solo exhibition in New York. Produces sparse paintings based on his poems. Meets Ross Bleckner, Guillermo Kuitca and Not Vital. Starts work related to Joan of Arc. The Museum of Contemporary Art, Hawaii and The

Bronx Museum of the Arts, New York, acquire paintings. Destroys all work related to Joan of Arc at the Daniel Arvizu Gallery. Moves to Venice, California.

1997

Begins creating environments that show dissimilar work. Reintroduces the figure. *Bird* acquired by The Palm Springs Museum. For the first time shows works on paper independent of the paintings. Writes book of poems and paintings. Makes works inspired by Saint Catherine and memory. Visits Berlin and begins a poem about his visit. Works on his first series of etchings and monotypes with printer John Armstrong, from Arizona. Meets Alexandra Williams. The Arizona State University Museum acquires the monotype series, *Icarus*.

1998

First solo exhibition in Europe. The Arkansas Art Center acquires *Unsafe*, a large work on paper. Finishes the poem *Berlin*. Concludes series of paintings, sculptures and photographs based on the poem. Is invited to exhibit in Vienna, Berlin, Paris and Caracas. Los Angeles County Museum of Art acquires the painting *Acceptance of Longing*.

1999

The idea of forgetfulness and image erosion prevails in the work. Creates large scale paintings for shows in London and Los Angeles. Marries Alexandra Williams. The Houston Museum of Fine Arts, Frederick R. Weisman Art Museun and the Sheldon Memorial Art Gallery acquire photographs. Upcoming solo museum exhibition at the Museum of Comtemporary Art, Hawaii, and exhibitions at the Los Angeles County Museum, and The Contemporary Museum, Baltimore.

Circumstance (In progress) 1997 ▶

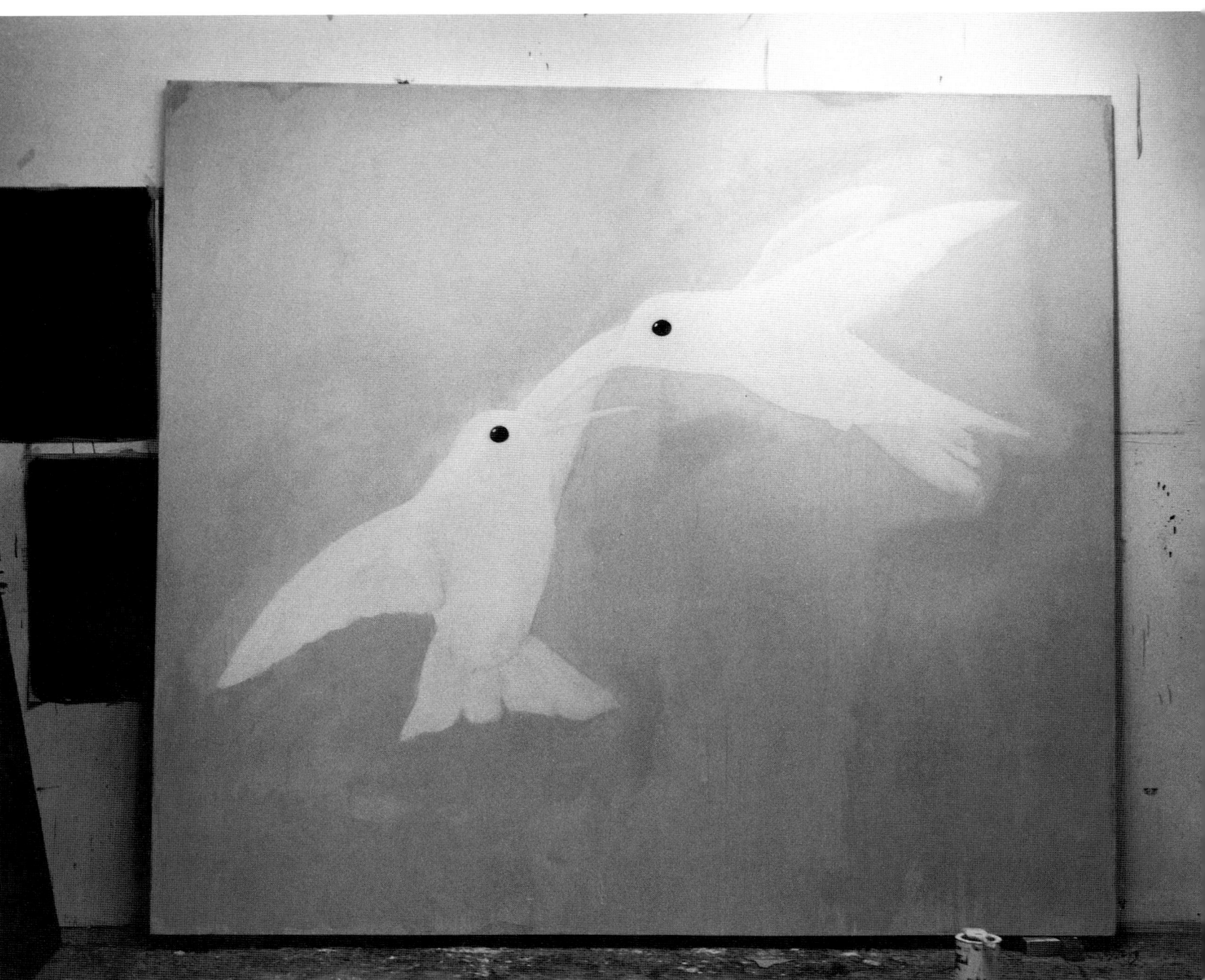

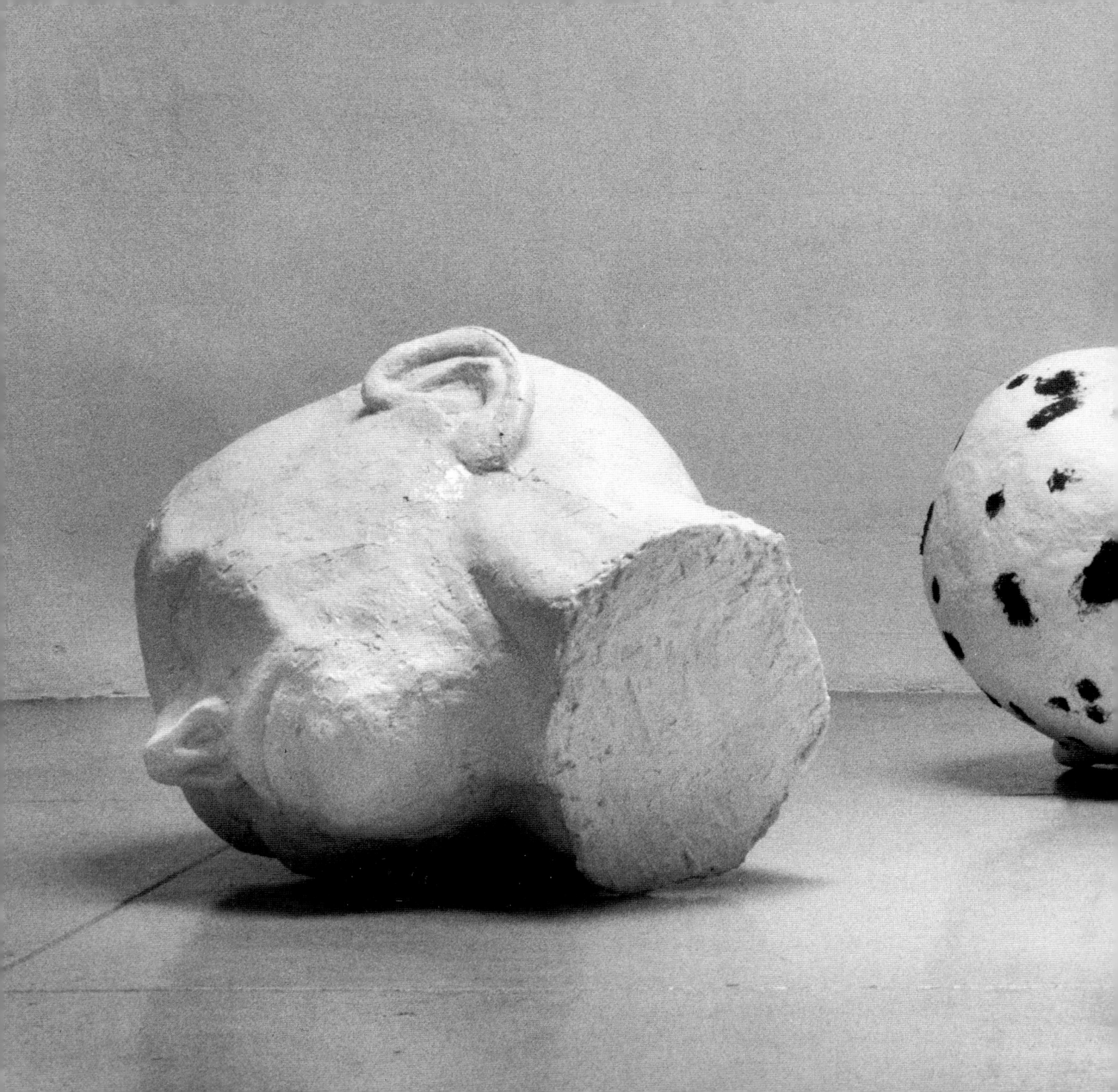

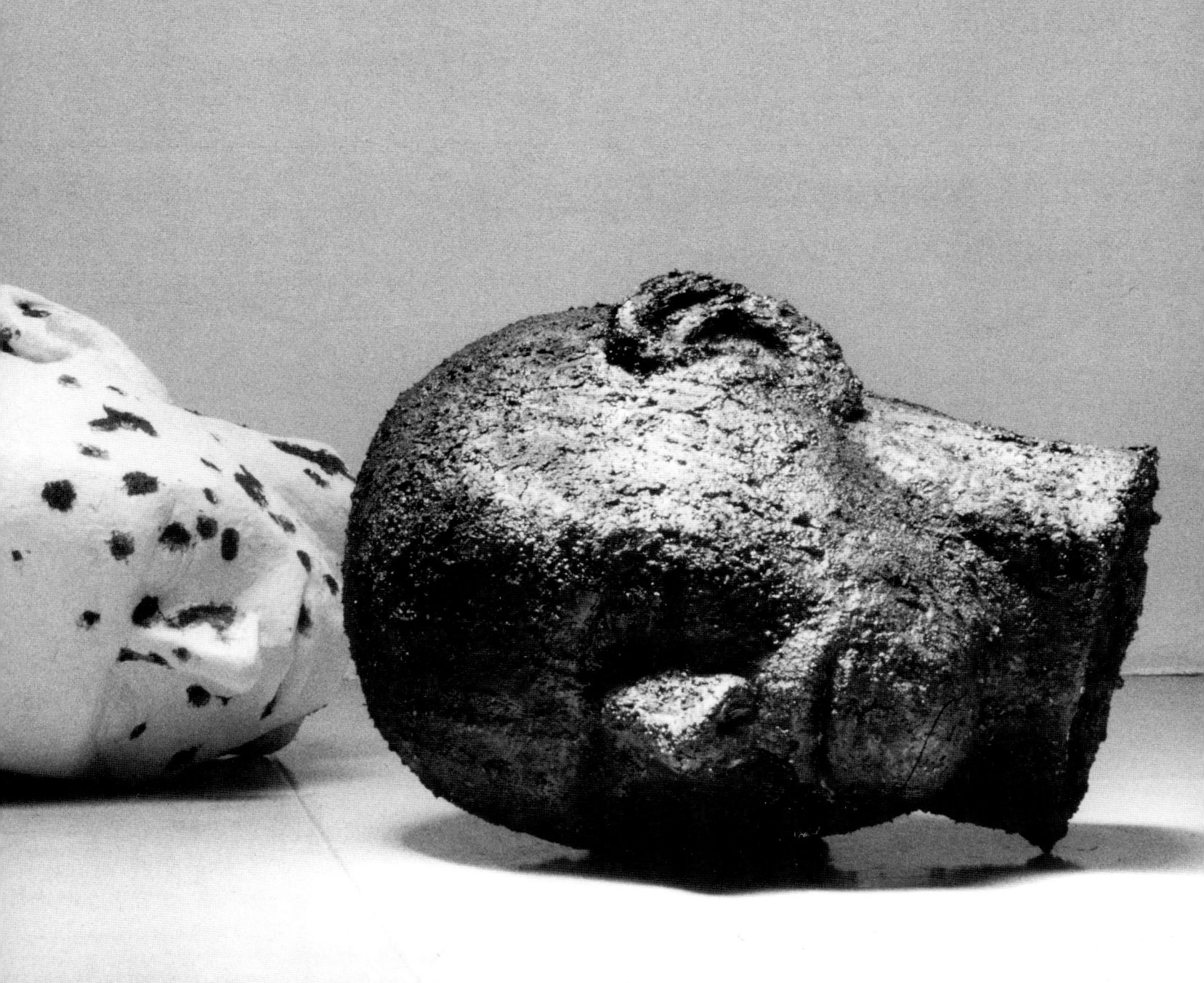

Exhibition History

Information regarding exhibitions listed in descending sequence, according to city, exhibition site, title of the exhibition, and details of catalog, if one exists. For a complete list of catalogs and books please refer to the section *Books, Artist's Publications and Solo Exhibition Catalogs.* Each exhibition is followed by a selection of the most important reviews.

Solo Exhibitions

1999

Andrew Mummery Gallery, London, United Kingdom.

Griffin Contemporary Exhibitions, Venice, California.

ARCO, Cutting Edge, Madrid, Spain.

1998

Griffin Contemporary Exhibitions, Venice, California. Catalog with text by Abigail Solomon-Godeau, Peter Frank and M.A. Greenstein.

- Leah Ollman, *Art in America*, May 1999, p. 166;
- Suvan Geer, *Art Nexus*, April-June 1999, pp. 131-132;
- Claudine Isé, *Los Angeles Times*, October 30, 1998, p. 30;

Galerie Bäumler, Regensburg, Germany.

- Er Will Bewegen, "No Entertaining! Enrique Martinez Celaya in der Regensburger Galerie Baumler," *Mittelbaycrische Zeitung*, June 30;

- Helmut Hein, "Atemwende oder Die Welt im Kopf," *Kultur, Mittelbaycrische Zeitung*, August 8;

Stephen Cohen Gallery, Los Angeles, California. Catalog.

- Leah Ollman, *Los Angeles Times*, December 25, p. F-40

Rena Bransten Gallery, San Francisco, California.

Baldwin Gallery, Aspen, Colorado.

- Carrie Click, "Sultan, Celaya debut Baldwin's new space," *Aspen Times*, February 14, p. 14B.

1997

Griffin Contemporary Exhibitions, Venice. Catalog.

- Peter Frank, *ArtNews*, February, p. 123;
- Staff, "Enrique Martínez Celaya, *Art Scene*, Oct 28-Nov 4.

Burnett Miller Gallery, Santa Monica, California.

- P.Y, "Enrique Martínez Celaya," *Buzz Weekly* (Los Angeles), Jan 31-Feb 6, p. 14;
- Eleonore Welles, "Enrique Martínez Celaya,"*Art Scene*, February, Vol. 6 No. 7.

Galeria Luigi Marrozzini, San Juan, Puerto Rico. Catalog.

- Enrique Garcia Gutierrez, "El artista en su laberinto, ", *En Nuevo Dia, Revista Domingo*, September 21, pp. 10-13;
- Manuel Alvarez Lezama, *San Juan Star*, October 3;
- Mario Alegre Barrios, *El Nuevo Dia*, Sept 2.

Galerie Douyon, Miami, Florida.

- Carol Damian, *Art Nexus*, January-March, pp. 132-133;
- Rodolfo Windhausen, "Arte Latinoamericano," *La Prensa*, November 23.

- Armando Alvarez Bravo, *El Nuevo Herald* (Miami), November 2, p. 5E.

1996

Tricia Collins • Grand Salon, New York, New York. Catalog with text by Charles A. Riley.

Rena Bransten Gallery, San Francisco, California.

Bronx Museum of the Arts(2), Bronx, New York. Catalog with text by Marysol Nieves.

Daniel Arvizu Gallery, Santa Ana, California. Catalog.

- Rebecca Schoenkopf, "A Marriage in Blood," *OC Weekly* (Orange County), August 9, p. 25.

1995

Dorothy Goldeen Gallery, Santa Monica, California.

- David A. Greene, "Painting the Town," *Los Angeles Reader*, September 29.

1994

Ro Snell Gallery, Santa Barbara, California. Catalog with text by Stephen Westfall.

- Paul Von Froemming, "Gifts of Love," *The Independent* (Santa Barbara), December 1, p. 58;
- Joan Crowder, "Drawing the Viewers Into His Personal Drama," *Santa Barbara News Press*, November 25, p. 63.

Meridian Gallery, San Francisco, California. Catalog with text by Stephen Westfall.

- Steven Jenkins, "An Open Heart," *Artweek*, November 17, 1994.

University Art Museum, Santa Barbara, California. Catalog.

- Michael Darling, "The Graduate," *Scene Magazine* (Santa Barbara), April 29, pp. 23-24;
- Chris George, *Arts Week: Daily Nexus* (Santa Barbara), May 19, p. 4;
- Judith Callander, *The Independent* (Santa Barbara), May 19, 1994, p. 50.

1993

Galeria Botello, San Juan, Puerto Rico. Catalog with text by Michael Darling.

- Manuel Alvarez Lezama, "Exhibit Asks Viewers to Question Boundaries," *The San Juan Star*, April 7, p. F11;
- "Arte," *El Nuevo Dia* (San Juan, Puerto Rico), March 23;
- Eneid Routte-Gomez, *The San Juan Star* (San Juan), March 23.

1992

Sunnyvale Art Center, Sunnyvale, California. Catalog with text by Patrice Wagner.

- Derk Richardson, "Eight Days a Week," *San Francisco Bay Guardian;*
- Dorothy Burkhart, "An Artist Worth Being Excited About," *San Jose Mercury News*, March 18, p. 7D.

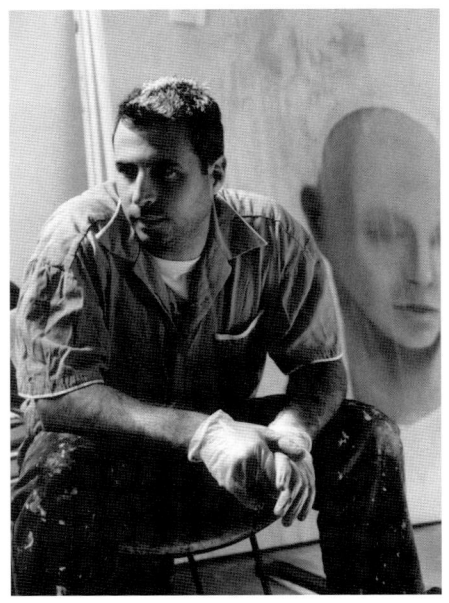

Selected Group Exhibitions

1999

"The Contemporary Collection," Los Angles County Museum of Art, Los Angeles

Museo de las Americas, "Pequeño Formato 98.99," San Juan, Puerto Rico. Catalog.

- Jose Antonio Perez Ruiz, *Art Nexus*, May, pp. 132-133;

Galerie Bäumler, Regensburg, Germany.

1998

Weatherspoon Art Gallery, "Art on Paper," University of North Carolina, Greensboro.

Arkansas Art Center, "National Drawing Invitational," Little Rock, Arkansas.

Charles Cowles Gallery, New York, New York.

Rare Gallery, "Pulse, Painting Now," New York, New York.

Rare Gallery, "California Current," New York, New York.

1997

The Contemporary Museum, "The Permanent Collection," Honolulu, Hawaii.

Contemporary Arts Forum, Santa Monica, California.

Andrew Mummery/33 Great Sutton Street, London, United Kingdom.

George Adams Gallery, New York, New York.

Tricia Collins • Grand Salon, "Conversions," New York, New York.

Rena Bransten Gallery, "Pool," San Francisco, California.

1996

Triton Museum of Art, "Drawings: Realism to Abstraction," Santa Clara, California.

Museum of Contemporary Art, Annual Auction, Santa Monica, California.

Reed's Wharf Gallery, London, United Kingdom.

Carla Stellweg Gallery, New York, New York.

1995

Santa Barbara Museum of Art, "Re-Inventing the Avant-Garde: Modernism and the Art of Latin America," Santa Barbara, California. Catalog with text by Diana Dupont.

- Joan Crowder, "A Vision with Two Views," *Santa Barbara News Press*, December 8, pp. 7-8.

Newport Harbor Art Museum, Newport Beach, California.

Museo Regional de Arte y Cultura, Palos, Cuba.

Laguna Gloria Art Museum, "New American Talent: The Eleventh Exhibition," Austin, Texas.

Irvine Fine Arts Center, "Nature re(Contained)," Irvine, California.

1994

Chattahoochee Valley Art Museum, "Lagrange XVIII National Biennial," Lagrange, Georgia.

Cheekwood Museum of Art, "National Contemporary Painting Exhibition," Nashville, Tennessee.

Laguna Gloria Art Museum, Austin, Texas.

Texas A & M University Gallery, College Station, Texas

Los Angeles Municipal Art Gallery, Los Angeles, California.

1993

Brown County Museum, Brownwood, Texas.

Ro Snell Gallery, Santa Barbara, California.

-Michael Darling, "Viewing Works Together, Singularly," *Santa Barbara News Press*, October 11.

Plainview Cultural Arts Council, Plainview, Texas.

1992

Oakland Museum, Oakland, California.

R.B. Stevenson Gallery, La Jolla, California.

1991

Corvallis Art Center, Corvallis, Oregon.

Galeria Botello, San Juan, Puerto Rico.

1979

Liga de Arte de San Juan, San Juan, Puerto Rico.

General Reference Articles and Interviews

Judy Perez, "Art on the Fringes," *Claremont Courier*, April 10, p. 9, 1999;

Tricia Collins, curator, "Tablet, the work of three poets," *ZingMagazine*, Winter, pp. 134-138, 1998;

Dru Hilty, "Art and Features," *The Student Life*, Pomona College, October 30, p. 4, 1998;

T.W Brown, (Photo), *The Argonaut*, May 14, p. 23, 1998;

Staff, *Mittelbayerische Zeitung*, June 28, p. R6, 1998;

Christopher Miles, *Art Week*, December, p. 17, 1997;

Nina Ellerman, "Self-portrait with Cup," *Pomona College Magazine*, Spring, pp. 24-31, 1997;

Michael Darling, "An Unusually Rich Storehouse of Ideas," *Scene Magazine* (Santa Barbara), August, 1993;

Pam O'Connell, "Arts Beat," *Billboard: Express* (Berkeley), May 8, p. 33, 1991;

Mario Alegre, "Profuso y cálido cromatismo en Martínez Celaya," *El Nuevo Dia* (San Juan, Puerto Rico), June 28, 1991;

Stalks, California, poetry magazine featuring Enrique Martínez Celaya's drawings, Fall 1991.

Books, Artist's Publications and Solo Exhibitions Catalogs

Berlin, Los Angeles, Stephen Cohen Gallery, 1998;

Berlin, The Fragility of Nearness, Venice, Griffin Cotemporary, 1998. Texts by Abigail Solomon-Godeau, Peter Frank and M.A. Greeenstein;

Enrique Martínez Celaya, New York, Tricia Collins, Grand Salon, 1996. Text by Charles A. Riley;

Nature re(Contained), Irvine, Irvine Fine Arts Center, 1995. Text by Dorrit Rawlins;

Lions of Frosting, Santa Monica, Dorothy Goldeen Gallery, 1995. Text by Frances Pohl;

Presents and Proofs, San Francisco and Santa Barbara, Meridian Gallery and Ro Snell Gallery, 1994. Text by Stephen Westfall;

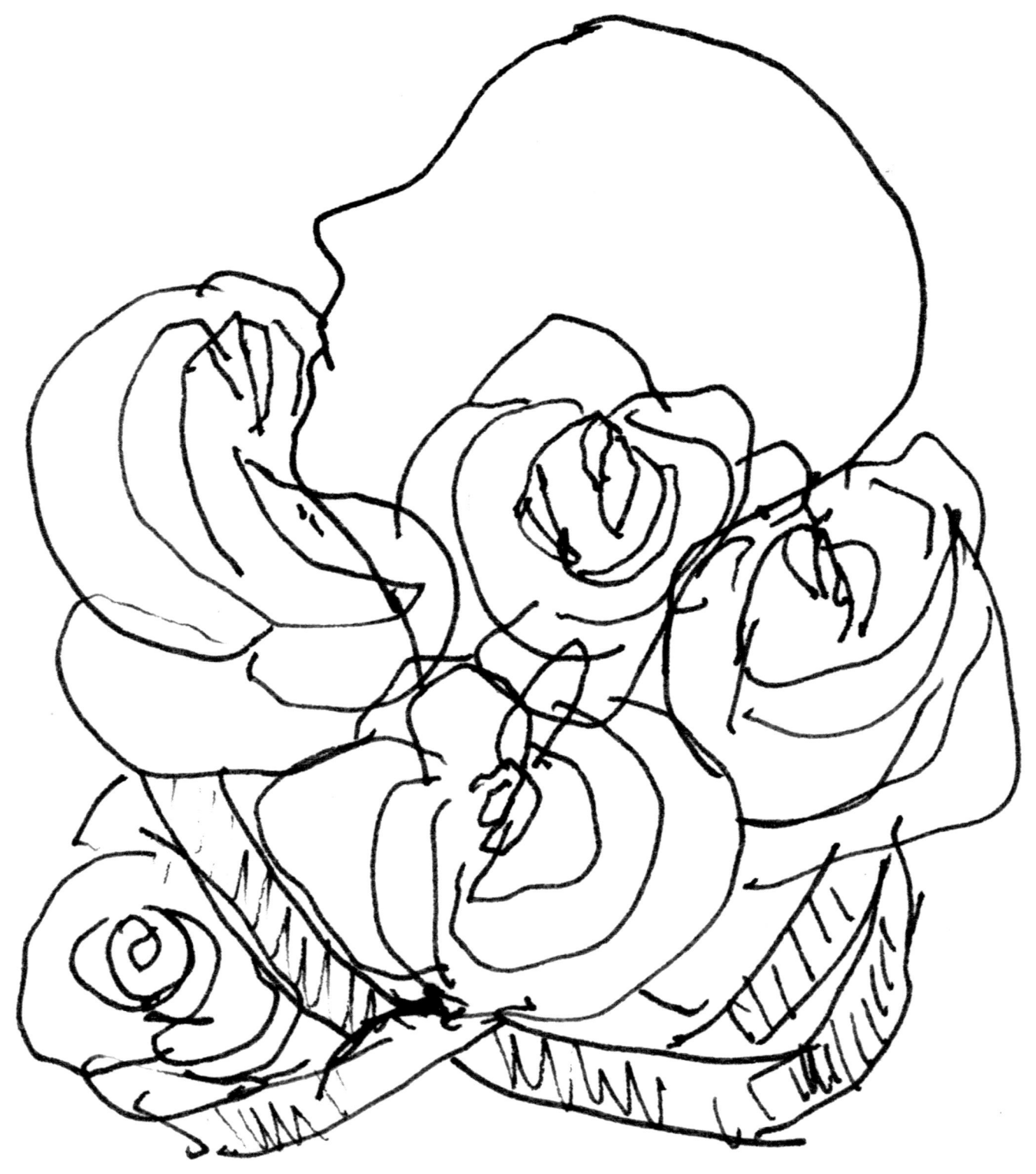

The Black Paintings, Santa Barbara, University Art Museum, 1994;

New American Talent, Austin, Texas, Laguna Gloria Art Museum, 1993. Text by Kerry Brougher;

Enrique Martínez Celaya, Sunnyvale, Sunnyvale Arts Center, 1992. Text by Patrice Wagner;

Enrique Martínez Celaya, *Poems for the Bed*, Berkeley, Albee Press, 1991;

Enrique Martínez Celaya, *Guthrie*, Berkeley, Albee Press, 1989.

Selected Public Collections

Los Angeles County Museum of Art, Los Angeles, California;

Neues Stadtmuseum der Stadt Landsberg/Lech, Germany;

The Contemporary Museum, Honolulu, Hawaii;

The Museum of Fine Arts, Houston, Texas;

The Bronx Museum of the Arts, Bronx, New York;

Palm Springs Desert Museum, Palm Springs, California;

Arkansas Art Center, Little Rock, Arkansas;

Sammlung und Privatmuseum Martin Scheuerer, Germany;

Arizona State University Museum, Phoenix, Arizona;

Frederick R. Weisman Art Museum, Minneapolis, Minnesota;

Sheldon Memorial Art Gallery, University of Nebraska, Lincoln, Nebraska.

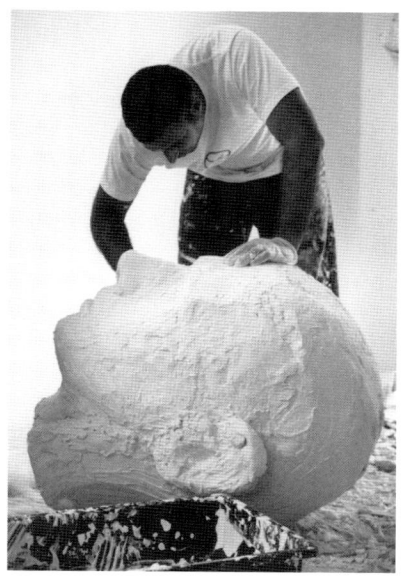

Quiet Night (ocean), Marina del Rey, California, 1999 ▶

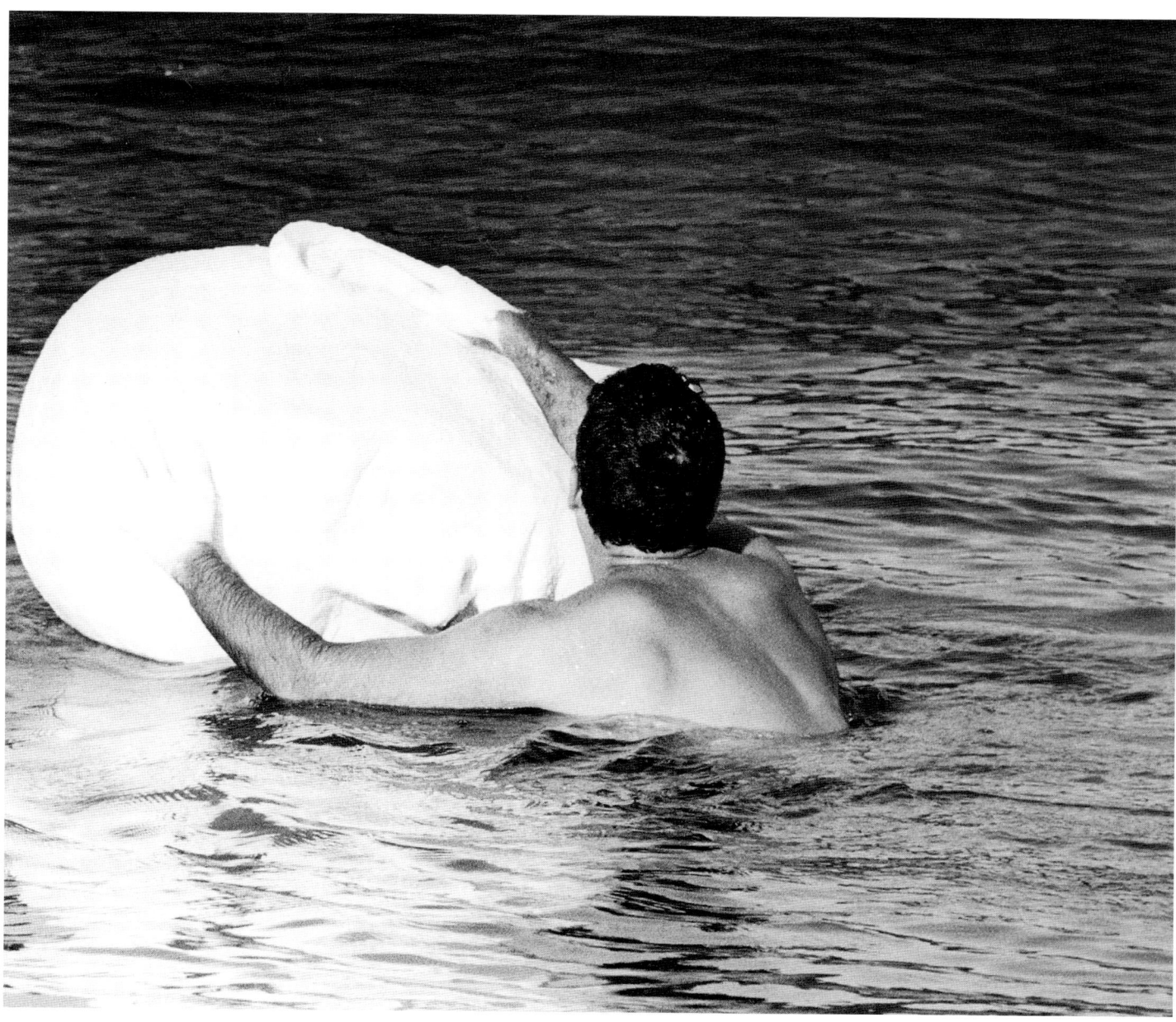

The great wait 1998 ▶

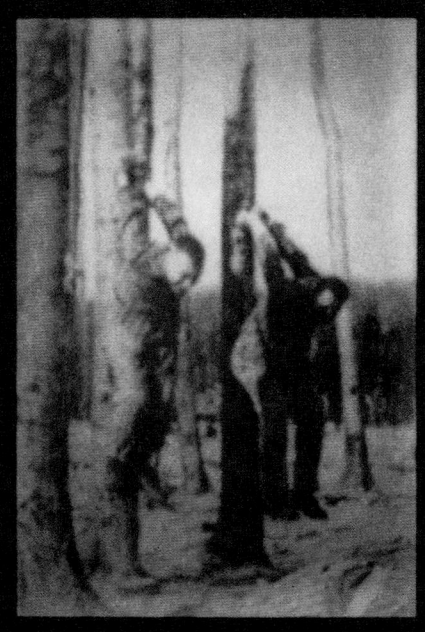

Do you miss me?

This monograph was created to celebrate the Enrique Martínez Celaya exhibitions held in October 1999 at Griffin Contemporary, Venice and at the St. Pancras Chambers Building/Andrew Mummery Gallery, London with the patronage of London and Continental Railways.

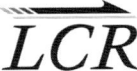

The exhibition at the former Midland Hotel at the St. Pancras Chambers Building was arranged by the Andrew Mummery Gallery and KP Productions with the generous support of the London and Continental Railways, the London and Continental Stations and Property Ltd., Stephen Jordan, and Leszek Dobrovolsky.

Author's Acknowledgements

Thanks to my father, Paul Graham Trueblood for teaching me to trust outbreaks of the spirit, to Enrique Martínez Celaya for his generousity of mind and for sharing his private sketchbooks and his works in progress, to Gabriela Loza for the sensitive transcriptions of some of the interviews, to Bill Griffin for his encouragement and to Molly Aine Moore for her wisdom and commitment in helping me prepare the manuscript.

Artist's Acknowledgements

I would like to take this opportunity to thank everyone who emotionally or financially have supported my work; it would have been hard to continue without them. I am deeply grateful to Anne Trueblood Brodzky for her belief in my work. I would like to thank Katherine Priestley, Wendy Simpson, Andrew Mummery and Bill Griffin for everything that they have done on behalf of the book, the exhibitions and my work. I am grateful to Pomona College and the Research Committee for their support of my work. I also would like to thank my shelter and my strength, my wife Alexandra.

Publisher's Acknowledgements

We would like to thank the following people and institutions for their support for this publication: Anne Trueblood Brodzky, Dr. Amnon Yariv, Donald Baechler, Katherine Priestley, Wendy Simpson, Andrew Mummery Gallery, London and Griffin Contemporary, Venice. Special thanks are due to David Minner, John Gullotti, Joanna Miller, Molly Aine Moore and Elizabeth Williams for their assistance in the preparation of materials. We would like to warmly thank Enrique Martínez Celaya for his constant help and patience in the development of this project.

Copy Editor: Meredith McDaniel.
Design: Working Graphics, Los Angeles with Anne Trueblood Brodzky and Enrique Martínez Celaya.
Photographs: Gene Ogami, Danny First, Charles Cowles and Enrique Martinez Celaya.
Printed and bound by: Typecraft, Inc., Pasadena.
Set in Garamond and Arena.
Printed in the United States of America.
First Edition 1999.

Whale and Star Press, Venice, California 90294-2192
www.whaleandstar.com
© 1999 Whale and Star Press
All works of Enrique Martínez Celaya are © Enrique Martínez Celaya.
All works are in private collections unless otherwise stated.

ISBN 0-9673608-0-3
Library of Congress Catalog Card Number: 99-65745

Facing page:
Leonardo 1999

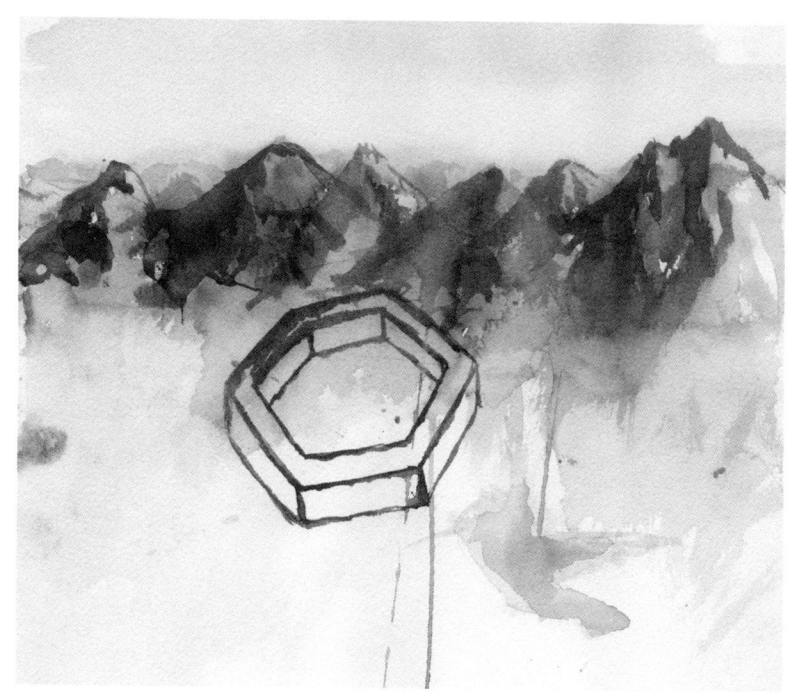